WHATEVER
Happened TO
FAITH?

ALSO BY ROBERT L. MILLET

Precept upon Precept

Men of Covenant

Living in the Millennium

Living in the Eleventh Hour

Lehi's Dream

Making Sense of the Book of Revelation

Talking with God

Men of Influence

Holding Fast

Men of Valor

What Happened to the Cross?

Are We There Yet?

Getting at the Truth

Grace Works

When a Child Wanders

WHATEVER
Happened TO
FAITH?

ROBERT L. MILLET

DESERET
BOOK

Salt Lake City, Utah

Library of Congress Cataloging-in-Publication Data

Names: Millet, Robert L., author.
Title: Whatever happened to faith? / Robert L. Millet.
Description: Salt Lake City, Utah : Deseret Book, [2017] | Includes bibliographical references and index.
Identifiers: LCCN 2017006730 | ISBN 9781629723334 (hardbound : alk. paper)
Subjects: LCSH: The Church of Jesus Christ of Latter-day Saints—Doctrines. | Mormon Church—Doctrines.
Classification: LCC BX8635.3 .M563 2017 | DDC 230/.9332—dc23
LC record available at https://lccn.loc.gov/2017006730

Printed in the United States of America
Publishers Printing, Salt Lake City, UT

10   9   8   7   6   5   4   3   2   1

To my grandfather Anatole J. Millet
a twentieth-century pioneer, a serious student of scripture
and preacher of righteousness, who received the
restored gospel enthusiastically and
defended it courageously

When the Son of man cometh, shall
he find faith on the earth?

—Luke 18:8

Stand fast, ye Saints of God, hold on a little
while longer, and the storm of life will be past, and you
will be rewarded by that God whose servants you are, and
who will duly appreciate all your toils and afflictions for
Christ's sake and the Gospel's. Your names will be
handed down to posterity as Saints of God.

—Joseph Smith

CONTENTS

PREFACE

As prophets have done in past dispensations, the leaders of the Church continue to call upon us to exercise faith in the Lord Jesus Christ, faith in his plans and purposes, faith in his divine timetable, faith in his Church and its prophetic and apostolic leadership. Exercising faith is not easy to do in our day, since we now live and breathe and have our being in the midst of a world largely drenched in secularity, a day when religion and religious devotion are being pushed to the margins of our society. Religious belief is scoffed at and denounced as primitive, simple-minded, unnecessary, even dangerous. Children and adults are taught to give little attention to the spiritual, to believe only in that which they can see and feel and measure. Loyalty to scriptural teachings, adherence to time-honored values and absolute truths—these qualities and virtues seem to be in short supply.

To exercise faith as Latter-day Saints in these early decades of the twenty-first century requires us to hold tenaciously to what we have been taught, what we have learned concerning the divine Sonship of Christ, the restoration of the fulness of the gospel and the Church of Jesus Christ, and the Savior's continued guidance of the "true and living church" (D&C 1:30).

Our Lord has charged us as his disciples to be in the world but not of it (John 17:14–15). It's tough to be the salt of the earth or the light of the world if in times of stress we persistently retreat from the world into the comfort of our bunkers of faith (Matthew 5:13–14; 3 Nephi 12:13–14). "Faith has always been a fundamental principle of strength for the Latter-day Saints," President Thomas S. Monson taught. "Without it, we go nowhere. With it, we can accomplish anything in building the kingdom of God."[1]

Our own people have not been immune to doubt, uncertainty, and troubles when it comes to matters of faith. The almost infinite spread of information (good and bad, true and false) by means of the Internet seems to have caught a number of Saints off guard. The decision of Church leaders in recent years to adopt a position of total transparency relative to our doctrine and history, perhaps most obviously manifest in the production of the Joseph Smith Papers, has proven for some Church members to be a godsend, filling in gaps of personal understanding and painting a picture of the Restoration that is rich and rewarding. For others in the Church, however, the discovery of historical details of which they had been unaware, combined with current positions of The Church of Jesus Christ of Latter-day Saints on sensitive and difficult matters pertaining to marriage, family, and sexual orientation, have been disturbing. Some declare that their faith in the Church and its leaders has been shaken. Add to these stressful items the continuing barrage of anti-Mormon propaganda from Christian groups or from former Latter-day Saints who have become bitter enemies of the faith, and the result is what might be called a perfect storm. The day for ignoring such matters is long since past.

I do not intend in this short work to address every doctrinal or historical challenge with which members wrestle, although we will of necessity touch on some. Instead, I'd like to direct our attention toward some guiding principles that, if understood, may allow some of us to see the Church—its doctrine, its history, and its leaders—with new eyes and perhaps feel with a new heart. What is my intended audience for this book? Well, it would certainly include the following:

- Active, involved, and committed members of the Church who have no reservations whatsoever about the faith. To this group I would hope to provide some measure of inoculation should they encounter tough issues in the future.

- Active and involved members of the Church who have encountered questions or issues that now trouble them.

- Members of the Church who have allowed themselves to slide into inactivity because of doctrinal or historical issues, current Church policies on social issues, or disappointment with Church leaders past and present.

- Former Latter-day Saints who have formally cut their ties with the Church and have charted a new course in life but feel no inclination to criticize or oppose the Church.

- Former Latter-day Saints who have formally cut their ties with the Church but are so angry about their feelings of "deception" and "betrayal" that they seem driven to do anything they can to embarrass, humiliate, or block the progress of the Church.

I have a deep and abiding conviction of the truthfulness of the restored gospel, its doctrine and history, and the integrity of the prophets and apostles of the restored Church. I am not unaware of the potentially troubling issues afloat. Yet nothing I have read or encountered has even come close to shaking my faith. Fortunately, many, many people within the Church feel the same, persons who are neither naïve nor unwilling to face reality. Rather, they have chosen the way of faith. As President Monson put it, "Whereas doubt destroys, faith fulfills. It brings one closer to God and to His purposes. Faith implies a certain trust—even a reliance—upon the word of our Creator."[2]

In preparing this work, I am indebted to many persons who were willing to engage in lengthy conversations on a myriad of tough issues and others who read portions of the manuscript and made valuable suggestions. Although such assistance was extremely helpful, even crucial, I alone am responsible for the conclusions drawn. This volume is a private endeavor and not a publication of either The Church of Jesus Christ of Latter-day Saints or of Brigham Young University.

Chapter 1

THE SIFTING
HAS BEGUN

At this stage of my life, I frequently forget to take my wallet or
mobile phone when I leave home. I'm delighted to see old
and beloved friends, but for some reason their names sometimes
escape me. Nevertheless, my memories of the year 1961, when
our family began attending meetings in the newly organized
branch of the Church in Baker, Louisiana, remain vivid. It was a
small gathering of Latter-day Saints who met in those formative
years in the girls' gymnasium of the high school. Those wonderful brothers and sisters were people of faith, men and women who
had paid a dear price to know what they knew.

Even then, as a young and restless teenager, I felt something
deep down as I listened to simple but heartfelt talks in sacrament
meeting, participated in Sunday School lessons, and heard tender
expressions of conviction in fast and testimony meetings. I will
go to my grave recalling the sweet testimonies of members of the
branch, especially the older and more seasoned ones. Over the
years, as I attended carefully to the testimonies of these persons, I
longed for the day when I could know as they knew, when I would
be strong enough and convinced enough to stand and bear my own
testimony, when I would not need to lean on the witness of others.

Even though the testimonies borne from month to month

1

were not what one could describe as original—the Saints basically said much the same each time—they were unique in that each of those people had come to faith in a distinctive manner, and so each one's particular expressions moved and motivated me in different ways. One phrase was used quite often by several of the older members of the congregation. They would often end their remarks by encouraging us to "endure to the end," for, they would add, a "day of sifting is coming." It sounded to me like some kind of warning. Being a city boy myself, I had no idea what *sifting* meant or how something or someone could be sifted. I just knew it sounded bad, something I probably didn't want to happen to me.

A Test Is Coming

When I returned home from the Eastern States Mission and transferred to Brigham Young University, I dived headlong into my religion classes feeling much like a giddy child in a candy store. I also began to collect important Church books to build my library. I started with the teachings and biographies of the Presidents of the Church and then worked my way through the early apostles. I had read *The Autobiography of Parley P. Pratt* while on my mission. I came eventually to Orson F. Whitney's *Life of Heber C. Kimball,* and as I read that marvelous volume, I was moved by Heber's unflinching devotion to the Prophet Joseph Smith and the cause of the Restoration.

When I came to the year 1856 in Heber's story, I encountered a prophetic warning uttered by Brother Kimball. "We think we are secure here in the chambers of the everlasting hills," he observed, "where we can close those few doors of the canyons against mobs and persecutors, the wicked and the vile, who have always beset us . . . , but I want to say to you, my brethren, the time is coming when we will be mixed up in these now peaceful valleys to that extent that it will be difficult to tell the face of a Saint from the face of an enemy to the people of God." Then came this chilling remark: "Then, brethren, *look out for the great sieve, for there will be a great sifting time, and many will fall; so I say unto you there is a test, a TEST, a TEST coming, and who will be able to stand?*"[1]

In 1867, not long before Heber's death, he sounded a similar warning: "Let me say to you, that many of you will see the time when you will have all the trouble, trial and persecution that you can stand, and plenty of opportunities to show that you are true to God and his work. *This Church has before it many close places through which it will have to pass before the work of God is crowned with victory.* To meet the difficulties that are coming, it will be necessary for you to have a knowledge of the truth of this work for yourselves. The difficulties will be of such a character that the man or woman who does not possess this personal knowledge or witness will fall. If you have not got the testimony, live right and call upon the Lord and cease not until you obtain it. If you do not you will not stand.

"Remember these sayings. . . . The time will come when no man or woman will be able to endure on borrowed light. Each will have to be guided by the light within himself. If you do not have it, how can you stand?"[2]

The Sifting of Souls

In the nearly half a century since I first read those haunting words, I have come to appreciate that the word *sift* may be used in many related ways. Each definition points toward a different way one may be sifted. Some synonyms for *sift* are *separate, distinguish, scatter, screen, strain, filter,* or *eliminate.* To sift is also to put a person to a test or trial.[3] We know, for example, of moments in ancient history when the children of Israel were sifted. Moses ascended Mount Sinai to commune with Jehovah, receive the Ten Commandments, and be instructed. The scriptural account indicates that he was gone for forty days. Now forty days is a long time for a people prone to mischief to be left alone.

And so it was that when the Lawgiver descended from Sinai, he discovered that the children of Israel had "corrupted themselves" and broken their covenant with God. The Old Testament account euphemistically states that the Israelites "rose up to play." In addition, they persuaded Aaron to make them a golden calf to worship. Seeing this debauchery among a people the Lord hoped to make a peculiar people, a kingdom of priests and priestesses, Moses was pained and filled with righteous indignation. "Then Moses stood in the gate of the camp, and said, *Who is on the Lord's side? let him come unto me*." Sadly, only the sons of Levi gathered to his side (Exodus 32:6–8, 19, 26; emphasis added). This tragic event was a sifting.

Half a millennium later, the prophet Elijah confronted king Ahab and Jezebel, his wife, and challenged the prophets of Baal to a kind of spiritual duel, intended to manifest plainly the omnipotence of Jehovah and the impotence of Baal. Elijah inquired of the people of Israel: "*How long halt ye between two opinions? if the LORD [Jehovah] be God, follow him: but if Baal, then follow him*" (1 Kings 18:21, 38–40; emphasis added). The word *halt* is a rather fascinating word to use in connection with Israel at that time. It means to walk lamely, to limp.[4] It also means to falter, to be hesitant, to be in doubt, to waver. This was for Israel a significant time of decision: would they cast their lot with the God of Abraham, Isaac, and Jacob, or would they turn instead to Baal? Once again, many of the Israelite chose unwisely. It was another time of sifting.

In the meridian of time, a rather dramatic time of sifting came after the Master's Bread of Life sermon, in which he taught in plain language: "I am the living bread which came down from heaven: if any man eat of this bread, he shall live for ever: and the bread that I will give is my flesh, which I will give for the life of the world." This was clearly a message intended to draw a line in the sand, to sift out those whose interest in Jesus Christ was shallow, perhaps no more than idle curiosity. Then the Master waxed even more direct: "Except ye eat the flesh of the Son of man, and drink his blood, ye have no life in you."

Those not in tune with the Spirit of God could neither discern the meaning nor perceive the profundity of the Savior's remarks. "Many therefore of his disciples, when they had heard this, said, This is an hard saying; who can hear it? . . . From that time many of his disciples went back, and walked no more with him." Then follows what for me is a poignant and even painful moment when the Promised Messiah turned to his beloved apostles and inquired: "*Will ye also go away?*" Peter responded powerfully: "Lord, to whom shall we go? thou hast the words of eternal life. And we believe and are sure that thou art that Christ, the Son of the living God" (John 6:51, 53, 60, 66–69; emphasis added). In this case, hard doctrine sifted out many who had a fascination with Jesus but had not discovered, by the power of the Spirit of God, who he was and what he had come to earth to do.

In referring to the latter days, Elder Bruce R. McConkie pointed out that a "testing and sifting process has ever been part of the Lord's system."[5]

The Waning of Faith

During my more than thirty years of teaching at Brigham Young University, I met with a number of young Latter-day Saint students who were spiritually troubled, who were wrestling with their faith. In my last five years at BYU, however, I listened to and counseled with more students who were angry, who felt "betrayed," and even a few who planned to leave the Church after graduation, than in the previous twenty-five years combined.

I found that some very real cultural and ideological factors are pressing upon the minds and hearts of the people of our day and time, distinctive and unusual factors that have contributed to a great deal of distress, soul searching, doubt, dejection, and even apostasy. How and in what manner are Latter-day Saints being sifted today?

Some of us seem to have forgotten (or perhaps overlooked) what it means to truly exercise faith in God our Heavenly Father and in his plan of salvation, in the Lord Jesus Christ and in his restored gospel. Further, some fail to have faith in the Lord's divine timetable, faith coupled with patience, trusting that the answers and assurances will eventually come. So many times when I have listened to acquaintances and even lifelong friends who now express disillusionment with Mormonism, treasured associates who are on the verge of leaving the faith of their fathers and mothers, I have respectfully held my tongue, when what I wanted most to do was cry out, "Whatever happened to faith? You once had faith. I know you did. I know that you once knew. Where did it go?"

Jesus spoke tenderly to Peter at the Last Supper: "Simon, Simon, behold, *Satan hath desired to have you, that he might sift you as wheat: But I have prayed for thee, that thy faith fail not:* and when thou art converted, strengthen thy brethren" (Luke 22:31–32; emphasis added). It should come as no great surprise to anyone that Satan, the father of lies, the master of deceit, the "accuser of our brethren" (Revelation 12:10), wants our souls; his desire is to sift us—to separate us, to scatter us, to filter us out, and, of course, to eliminate us spiritually. He is consummately miserable, and he is only too eager to share his misery (see 2 Nephi 2:18, 27). But would it be too much of a stretch to suggest that just as the Savior prayed for Peter, so the Savior is also praying for you and me, praying for our well-being, importuning and pleading to his Father and ours that our faith doesn't fail us?

The truth is, loved ones here on earth and loved ones in the postmortal spirit world are also praying that we will remain faithful, particularly at a time when so many are being lured away from faith. President George Albert Smith taught: "Think of the devotion and the faithfulness of those who day after day go into these temples and officiate for those who have passed to the other side; and know this, that *those who are on the other side are just as anxious about us. They are praying for us and for our success. They are pleading, in their own way, for their descendants, for their posterity who live upon the earth,* many of whom, because they have been unwise, have been betrayed into fighting the Church and kingdom of God and opposing those who are its leaders."[6]

The words of Jesus to his chief apostle suggest to us that when a man or woman is truly converted, wholly yielded to the Lord, His gospel, and His Church and kingdom, his or her faith *will not fail.* Such persons are truly built upon the Rock, and they are then in a position to lift and encourage others toward that real growth we know as deep conversion.

There is simply too much at stake to relinquish our hold on the iron rod. Too many people have given their lives, sacrificed their reputation in the world, forsaken all they have and all they are for the kingdom of God; too many tears have been shed on our behalf, too many pleading petitions have been sent heavenward, for any one of us to lose hope, to lose faith, to give up.

Conclusion

The older I get, the more I treasure the beloved hymns of Zion and stirring anthems of the Restoration. One hymn in particular, "Carry On," moves me to the core.[7] The chorus begins:

And we hear the desert singing:
Carry on, carry on, carry on!
Hills and vales and mountains ringing:
Carry on, carry on, carry on!

Almost always I stop singing at that point, not because I want to listen to the congregation, but because I am overcome with emotion. I see in my mind's eye Joseph Smith and Brigham Young and Emma Smith and Eliza R. Snow and Emmeline B. Wells and hosts of other early members of the Church; I see David O. McKay and Harold B. Lee and Belle S. Spafford and Barbara B. Smith laying it all on the altar, holding back nothing for the kingdom of God, even their own lives.

With the eye of faith, I see my grandfather Anatole, my own father, Albert, my aunt Gladys and uncle Joseph earnestly beckoning to me to carry on, to stay on track, to remain faithful, to maintain my place on the good ship *Zion*.[8] Our charge and our challenge are not to bury our heads in the sand as though there were no problems—no issues, no hard questions—but rather be willing to move forward in faith, knowing that if we can be patient, be a bit more trusting, and persist in our quest for truth, in the Lord's time and in his own way answers and resolutions will come to us. We will then be ever so grateful that we stayed with it and finished the course honorably.

Chapter 2

EXAMINE YOURSELVES

In his marvelous Sermon on the Mount, Jesus warned that "if thy right eye offend thee, pluck it out, and cast it from thee: for it is profitable for thee that one of thy members should perish, and not that thy whole body should be cast into hell. And if thy right hand offend thee, cut it off, and cast it from thee: for it is profitable for thee that one of thy members should perish, and not that thy whole body should be cast into hell" (Matthew 5:29–30).

That is fairly graphic, emphatic counsel by the Savior. It is a chilling warning. In his inspired translation of the Gospel of Mark, the Prophet Joseph Smith rendered Mark's version of these remarks as follows: "Therefore, if thy hand offend thee, cut it off; *or if thy brother offend thee and confess not and forsake not,* he shall be cut off. It is better for thee to enter into life maimed, than having two hands, to go into hell. For it is better for thee to enter into life without thy brother, than for thee and thy brother to be cast into hell; . . . and again, if thy foot offend thee, cut it off; *for he that is thy standard, by whom thou walkest, if he become a transgressor, he shall be cut off.*" Note the poignant summary of the matter: "Therefore, *let every man stand or fall, by himself, and not for another; or not trusting another*" (JST, Mark 9:40–42, 44; emphasis added).

Christ's message here is timely and timeless: while each of us can point to remarkable men and women whose examples, teachings, and way of life have powerfully influenced our own lives, persons whose faithfulness contributed markedly to the formation of our own faith, in the end every man and woman must know for themselves, must have a witness that is independent of others' convictions. In the end, we each rise or fall on our own. I cannot be saved on the basis of my parents' or grandparents' deep-seated faith. Just as the Lord's Church as an institution must "stand independent above all other creatures beneath the celestial world" (D&C 78:14), so the disciples of that Lord must receive their own spiritual confirmation of this work that enables them to stand tall in defense of the gospel, particularly if others should stumble or falter.

A Close Examination

One has only to do a casual reading of Paul's letters to his beloved Saints in the various branches of the Church to appreciate the challenges he and they faced. His letters were really regulatory correspondence, wise counsel from a loving apostle to his treasured converts to the Christian faith. One branch wrestled with the temptation to retain allegiance to the law of Moses; another struggled with Greek philosophy and culture. The Corinthian branch had a number of challenges, especially morality. Toward the end of his second epistle to the Corinthians, Paul assures the Saints that "though [Christ] was crucified through weakness, yet he liveth by the power of God. For we also are weak in him, but we shall live with him by the power of God toward you." Then comes this sobering directive: "*Examine yourselves, whether ye be in the faith;* prove your own selves" (2 Corinthians 13:4–5; emphasis added).

What are some ways that you and I might examine ourselves to determine if we are "in the faith," in harmony with the teachings and beliefs, the practices and daily life that accompany membership in The Church of Jesus Christ of Latter-day Saints? How would we prove ourselves? Mortality, life in this second estate, is an ongoing exercise of self-assessment, a regular, at least weekly (in our sacrament service), analysis of our thoughts, our feelings, and our behavior. Through this means we see things, especially about ourselves, as they really are. So very often we see things as *we* are and thus perceive only an approximation of what is, rather than seeing things through God's eyes, through the "mind of Christ" (1 Corinthians 2:16), the lens of the Lord. This lens is placed on our eyes, hearts, and minds as we cultivate the gift of the Holy Ghost in our lives. As I have reflected on this matter of examining myself to see if I am "in the faith," I have come up with a few points of assessment that I have found helpful:

1. *Do I hold—and do I use regularly—a current temple recommend?* I begin here because in so many ways my worthiness to attend the temple and participate in the covenants and ordinances there is a sure sign of the extent to which I am "in the faith." It is also a very effective indication of my readiness, my preparedness, to enter the celestial kingdom.

President Howard W. Hunter served as President of the Church for only a short time, but in those months he delivered to the Latter-day Saints penetrating words relative to the temple. "Let us truly be a temple-attending and a temple-loving people," he counseled us. "We should hasten to the temple as frequently, yet prudently, as our personal circumstances allow. We should go not only for our kindred dead but also for the personal blessing of temple worship, for the sanctity and safety that are within those hallowed and consecrated walls. As we attend the temple, we learn more richly and deeply the purpose of life and the significance of the atoning sacrifice of the Lord Jesus Christ."[1]

President Hunter also said: "I invite the Latter-day Saints to *look to the temple of the Lord as the great symbol of your membership. . . . The things that we must do and not do to be worthy of a temple recommend are the very things that insure we will be happy as individuals and as families."*[2] And, I would add, they are the very things that qualify us for entrance into the highest heaven hereafter. The temple represents God's earthly counterpart to paradise, the abode of the righteous in the postmortal spirit world. When someone is worthy to enter the House of the Lord, they are worthy to enter paradise at the time of death; they have been, as the revelation describes it, "quickened by a portion of the celestial glory" here and will, in the resurrection, "receive of the same, even a fulness" (D&C 88:29).

2. *Am I finding satisfaction and fulfillment in my Church membership?* Is belonging to the Church and participating in its programs enjoyable and uplifting to me? President Dieter F. Uchtdorf reflected: "I wonder if we as Church members might also benefit from asking ourselves from time to time: 'Is my experience in the Church working for me? Is it bringing me closer to Christ? Is it blessing me and my family with peace and joy as promised in the gospel?' . . .

"Many members will answer with great warmth that their experience as a member of the Church is working exceptionally well for them. . . . Every day I meet Church members who are filled with a radiant joy and who demonstrate in word and deed that their lives are immeasurably enriched by the restored gospel of Jesus Christ.

"But I also recognize that there are some who have a less-than-fulfilling experience. . . . This saddens me because I know firsthand how the gospel can invigorate and renew one's spirit—how it can fill our hearts with hope and our minds with light. I know for myself how the fruits of the gospel of Jesus Christ can transform lives from the ordinary and dreary to the extraordinary and sublime."[3]

I have heard it said that in some cases falling away from the Church is a lot like falling out of bed. One usually falls out of bed when one is not fully in the bed, close to the center. One who falls asleep on the edge of the mattress should not be surprised to wake up on the floor. When individuals express concern to me that they really do not enjoy going to Church meetings or participating in its auxiliaries or programs, I often ask about the level and depth to which they have previously been involved.

Elder L. Whitney Clayton of the Seventy explained that "we shouldn't be surprised when we suffer a failure of faith *if we walk on the margins of the strait and narrow path*. What we do and don't do really matters because actions have consequences, as does inaction. When we become inattentive to the small, daily, repetitive but essential actions of belief, we weaken our roots. Over time we slowly draw away from God.

"Thus, the way we speak to each other, the books and articles we read, the television shows and movies we watch, the things we don't read and would never watch, and the jokes we choose not to listen to or repeat all reflect where we are on the strait and narrow path—in the center or on the edges. We can't claim to be nourishing our roots if the things we do and don't do aren't calculated to make us better Saints. Safety is found only in the center of the strait and narrow path."[4]

Some years ago President Boyd K. Packer spoke at the funeral services for Sister Belle Spafford, General President of the Relief Society. He said that when the National Council of Women was organized in the 1870s, the Relief Society was one of the charter members. While serving on the general board of the Relief Society, Sister Spafford was assigned as the Church's delegate to their conventions in New York City. The Church in general and Sister Spafford in particular received little recognition or even acknowledgment, from the other members of that assembly. After one painful and difficult occasion during which she was basically ignored, if not shunned, by the women there, she returned home and scheduled an appointment with the prophet, President George Albert Smith. She firmly recommended to him that the Relief Society withdraw its membership from the National Council of Women, mentioning in particular the time and costs involved in participating. She added that, more than anything, "We don't get anything out of it."

Kindly, President Smith repeated her request to be sure he was hearing her correctly. She acknowledged that he did in fact understand her. President Smith then asked, "Tell me, please, Sister Spafford, what is it that you are putting into it?" The President instructed her to maintain Relief Society's membership in the National Council and charged her to make their influence felt.

Belle Spafford left the Prophet's office and went back to work with a new resolve. The Relief Society and The Church of Jesus Christ of Latter-day Saints continued to be represented in the National Council of Women for many years. The time came when Sister Spafford became General President of the Relief Society as well as president of the National Council. She also served as a delegate and officer in the International Councils.[5]

If a close and earnest examination of how much I am putting into my membership and involvement in the Church reveals that I am really, figuratively speaking, on the edge of the mattress, then perhaps I need to move closer to the center, evaluate whether my private devotions (personal scripture study, prayers, fasting, Church involvement, temple worship) are what they need to be. Superficial spiritual engagement seldom results in meaningful or even measurable spiritual growth. "Mormonism lite" generally produces a weak and shallow faith.

President Howard W. Hunter pointed out that "it is the general rule that we do not get things of value unless we are willing to pay a price. The scholar does not become learned unless he puts forth the work and effort to succeed. If he is not willing to do so, can he say there is no such thing as scholarship [or that there is no God]? . . . It is just as foolish for man to say there is no God simply because he has not had the inclination to seek him."[6] And so it is with gaining or reacquiring a testimony of the Restoration. Life as a social or cultural Latter-day Saint (much like that of a "nominal Christian" in the larger religious world) seldom brings a settled conviction, spiritual reassurance, or deep satisfaction that a steady and consistent gospel effort could produce.

3. *Am I in harmony with the leadership of the Church?* This item of personal assessment is especially important today. Practically every member of the Church who is active and involved has opportunity to raise their right arm to the square and manifest their sustaining vote of the apostles and prophets. That is easy enough to do when all is well, when there is no controversial social issue in the news. Most sing with gusto "We Thank Thee, O God, for a Prophet" until the leaders are bold enough to state that what a culture considers to be right and wrong is actually at cross-purposes with the mind of God.[7] We are supremely grateful to have seers and revelators at the head of the restored Church, as long, some members propose, as what they see and what they reveal is in complete harmony with what current society decrees.

It has been deeply disappointing, for example, to hear of members who are troubled, even angry when a Church authority announces that a recent decision by the Church on a sensitive social and family issue had come by revelation. What do prophets do? What do seers and revelators see and reveal, if they do not speak and act under the spirit of revelation? Elder Ronald A. Rasband, of the Quorum of the Twelve Apostles, taught: "We have sustained leaders today who, by divine inspiration, have been called to teach and guide us and who are calling out to us to beware of the dangers we face each day—from casual Sabbath-day observance, to threats to the family, to assaults on religious freedom, and *even to disputing latter-day revelation.* Brothers and sisters, are we listening to their counsel?"[8]

I am reminded of the words of Samuel the Lamanite, who spoke fearlessly atop the walls of Zarahemla: "If a man shall come among you and shall say: Do this, and there is no iniquity; do that and ye shall not suffer; yea, he will say: Walk after the pride of your own hearts; . . . and do whatsoever your heart desireth—and if a man shall come among you and say this, ye will receive him, and say that he is a prophet" (Helaman 13:27). Isn't that condemnation consistent with the apostle Paul's warnings that "the time will come when they will not endure sound doctrine; but after their own lusts shall they heap to themselves teachers, [the people] having itching ears; and they shall turn away their ears from the truth, and shall be turned unto fables" (2 Timothy 4:3–4). People have "itching ears" when they hear only what they want to hear.

Tragically, what too many want the prophets to do is either remain silent or see to it that they are in complete accord with the shifting sands of secular society. "The holy prophets have not only refused to follow erroneous human trends, but have pointed out these errors," President Spencer W. Kimball declared. "So often the prophets have been rejected because they first rejected the wrong ways of their own society." He continued: "Prophets have a way of jarring the carnal mind. . . . It is because of their love and integrity that *they cannot modify the Lord's message merely to make people feel comfortable. They are too kind to be so cruel.* I am grateful that prophets do not crave popularity."[9]

Early in this dispensation the Savior cautioned the Saints: "And all they who receive the oracles of God, let them beware how they hold them lest they are accounted as a light thing, and are brought under condemnation thereby" (D&C 90:5). Whether we cast our lot with the living prophets or take our cues from the loud and boisterous voices of the world will largely determine our spiritual standing in the kingdom of God—whether we are "in the faith." That choice will obviously determine, as well, how much we enjoy our Church membership.

4. *Am I in any way undermining the faith of other persons by what I say or do?*

President Henry B. Eyring spoke to religious educators about the need to exercise caution in how to teach and especially in what to teach. He referred to an instance in which a young woman named Kathy, who would eventually become his wife, had attended a religion class. The teacher often took a "devil's advocate" approach to the class to be sure that the students understood all sides of an issue. When Kathy confronted the instructor about his unusual manner of teaching, the teacher replied: "Well, I want to strengthen the students, and they will be stronger if they have to resolve these things themselves."

One student in particular who heard what was said in class spent much time trying to resolve the problems. A few years later President Spencer W. Kimball asked about that young man. President Eyring recalled: "Then he asked if I knew the teacher. Then he asked if I knew what was happening in the classroom. I answered yes to all of those questions. He said, 'Do you know where the student is now?' I answered, 'No.' He said, 'He's left the Church.' . . . President Kimball didn't say anything reproachful to me. . . . He just said these words that still are in my mind as clearly as if they were just spoken to me. They were not in anger, not even in rebuke. He just named the teacher and said, 'Oh! Oh, I'd hate to be him in the Judgment.'"[10]

We could continue on with this list at some length. We could discuss, for example, such questions as, Am I a builder or a murmurer, a sustaining influence or a naysayer? When the character or reputation of a Church leader is questioned, do I assume the best or the worst? When I am confronted by sensitive Church historical or doctrinal matters, do I approach them through the eyes of faith or the lenses of doubt? Is my faith and commitment to the restored gospel growing stronger and are my roots of faith going deeper? Is my approach to the Church and its doctrines intellectual only? Am I more concerned with having a stimulating conversation on a theological matter than I am in developing an abiding personal faith? Am I actively striving to follow the example of Jesus of Nazareth in my practice of pure religion? Because a testimony is like a muscle that needs to be exercised regularly, how often do I bear my testimony in public, particularly to my family and the ones I love? If I were arrested as a faithful and upstanding member of The Church of Jesus Christ of Latter-day Saints, would there be enough evidence to convict me?

An episode in the history of the Church teaches a valuable lesson about remaining in the faith. Elder B. H. Roberts wrote that in March 1837 Elder John Taylor visited Kirtland "and there met the Prophet Joseph Smith, who entertained him in his house and gave him many items of information pertaining to the work of the Lord in this dispensation. At that time there was a bitter spirit of apostasy rife in Kirtland. A number in the quorum of the Twelve were disaffected towards the Prophet, and the Church seemed on the point of disintegration. Among others, Parley P. Pratt was floundering in darkness, and coming to Elder Taylor told him of some things wherein he considered the Prophet Joseph in error. To his remarks Elder Taylor replied:

"'I am surprised to hear you speak so, Brother Parley. Before you left Canada [where Parley had taught the gospel to Brother Taylor] you bore a strong testimony to Joseph Smith being a Prophet of God, and to the truth of the work he has inaugurated; and you said you knew these things by revelation, and the gift of the Holy Ghost. You gave me a strict charge to the effect that though you or an angel from heaven was to declare anything else I was not to believe it.'" Note the gentle but direct chastisement by John Taylor: "Now Brother Parley, it is not man that I am following, but the Lord. The principles you taught me led me to Him, and I now have the same testimony that you then rejoiced in. *If the work was true six months ago, it is true today; if Joseph Smith was then a prophet, he is now a prophet.*" The account of this episode concludes with the comment that Parley and others of the brethren "were passing under a dark cloud; he soon made all right with the Prophet Joseph, and was restored to full fellowship."[11]

Conclusion

Joseph Smith summarized the need for introspective analysis with this charge: "Search your hearts, and see if you are like God. I have searched mine, and feel to repent of all my sins."[12] On another occasion he taught: "We ought to be willing to repent of and confess all of our own sins and keep nothing back."[13] It is always a good idea periodically to do some soul searching, to inquire as to one's spiritual depth, one's standing in the Lord's earthly kingdom. The apostle Paul's penetrating counsel for the members of the Church to examine themselves to determine whether they are "in the faith" may be as meaningful a charge in our day as at any time in the history of the Church of Jesus

Christ. In recent years, Latter-day Saints have been bombarded and buffeted with difficult questions, with criticisms and complaints, and with regular attacks on their faith. Unless we are rooted and grounded properly, we may not be able to stand. Once in a while it is not a bad question to ask: What would it take to shake me from my faith, dislodge me from the restored gospel, and send me searching for an alternative way of life? I am persuaded that as we seek earnestly to grow in faith, as we remain solidly involved as an active participant, as we live in a manner that the Holy Spirit of God is a consistent companion, we gradually begin to acquire a witness, a conviction, a testimony that is secure and unshakable (see Jacob 7:5; Enos 1:11). Doubt and uncertainty will no longer dog our steps. To that extent, we "enter into the rest of the Lord" (Alma 13:16).[14]

Chapter 3

THE DARK VEIL OF UNBELIEF

Ammon, the son of king Mosiah and a most successful missionary in ancient America, had a remarkable experience with king Lamoni. Ammon "knew that king Lamoni was under the power of God; he knew that *the dark veil of unbelief was being cast away from his mind,* and the light which did light up his mind, which was the light of the glory of God, which was a marvelous light of his goodness—yea, *this light had infused such joy into his soul, the cloud of darkness having been dispelled, and that the light of everlasting life was lit up in his soul,* yea, he knew that this had overcome his natural frame, and he was carried away in God" (Alma 19:6; emphasis added).

Questions and Doubts

It would be nearly impossible for a person living in our day, a time of information explosion, not to have questions about an array of things: Questions about certain events in the history of the Church, about specific Church leaders, about difficult doctrinal matters, and about the official position of The Church of Jesus Christ of Latter-day Saints on such sensitive issues as traditional marriage, sexual orientation, and religious liberty.

Questions arise. Why do we have questions, anyway? Consider

the following reasons: We are thinking. Our intellect is expanding. We are striving to love God with all our mind. Not everything has been revealed or discovered. We've not encountered everything yet. We have not paid a sufficient price to resolve the issue. We could be looking in all the wrong places. There are other things we need to learn first. We are human and thus limited in our perspective. Questions are a natural byproduct of being human. Questions, questions, and more questions—all around us. Questions are not, in other words, unusual, inappropriate, or a sign of weakness.

But what about doubts? What's the difference between having a question and doubting something? I consulted several dictionary definitions of *doubt* and found that it has changed very little in the last two centuries. Definitions of *doubt* in Webster's 1828 *American Dictionary of the English Language* include to waver or fluctuate in opinion, to hesitate, to hold questionable, to withhold assent from, to fear, to be apprehensive of, to suspect, to distrust, and to withhold confidence.[1] One can quickly see that doubt is a more serious form of questioning, a potentially more harmful form. Let's see how the word *doubt* is used in scripture.

After Peter had walked a short distance on the water, seeing the boisterous waves about him, he began to sink. "And immediately Jesus stretched forth his hand, and caught him, and said unto him, O thou of little faith, wherefore didst thou doubt?" (Matthew 14:31).

"Jesus answered and said unto them, Verily I say unto you, *If ye have faith, and doubt not,* ye shall not only do this which is done to the fig tree, but also if ye shall say unto this mountain, Be thou removed, and be thou cast into the sea; it shall be done" (Matthew 21:21; emphasis added).

"And seek not ye what ye shall eat, or what ye shall drink, neither be ye of doubtful mind" (Luke 12:29).

The stripling warriors "had been taught by their mothers, that if they did not doubt, God would deliver them. And they rehearsed . . . the words of their mothers, saying: We do not doubt our mothers knew it" (Alma 56:47–48). "And we do justly ascribe [their preservation] to the miraculous power of God, because of their exceeding faith in that which they had been taught to believe—that there was a just God, and whosoever did not doubt, that they should be preserved by his marvelous power" (Alma 57:26).

"And there were about three hundred souls who saw and heard these things [Nephi, Lehi, and a large group of people were "baptized by fire"]; and they were bidden to go forth and marvel not, neither should they doubt" (Helaman 5:49).

"Behold, I say unto you that whoso believeth in Christ, doubting nothing, whatsoever he shall ask the Father in the name of Christ it shall be granted him; and this promise is unto all, even unto the ends of the earth" (Mormon 9:21).

"And because of the knowledge of this man [the brother of Jared] he could not be kept from beholding within the veil; and he saw the finger of Jesus, which, when he saw, he fell with fear; for he knew that it was the finger of the Lord; and he had faith no longer, for he knew, nothing doubting" (Ether 3:19).

"Look unto me in every thought; *doubt not, fear not*" (D&C 6:36; emphasis added).

"He that doeth not anything until he is commanded, and receiveth a commandment with doubtful heart, and keepeth it with slothfulness, the same is damned" (D&C 58:29).

Members of the School of the Elders were taught that if God was not long-suffering and compassionate, loving and forgiving, "man would be cut off from before him, in consequence of which *he would be in continual doubt and could not exercise faith; for where doubt is, there faith has no power.*"[2] They were also instructed that if men and women do not trust in the truth that our Heavenly Father is a God of justice, "they [will] be filled with fear and doubt lest the judge of all the earth would not do right, and thus *fear or doubt* [note here how they are equated], existing in the mind, *would preclude the possibility of the exercise of faith* in him for life and salvation."[3]

I refer to so many of these statements because of how doubt is viewed and, from my perspective, misunderstood in our day. Evangelical Christian scholar Albert Mohler wrote: "Unsurprisingly, it is only after the Enlightenment that atheism became a real intellectual force. The Enlightenment produced a massive shift in the conditions of belief." He adds that "the result was a new opportunity for the denial of belief in the supernatural in general and the denial of a personal supernatural God specifically. *Doubt came to be considered as an intellectual tool, and there arose a culture of doubt and skepticism.* In the period from the sixteenth to the eighteenth century, the conditions of belief changed dramatically."[4]

We are the heirs of much Enlightenment thinking today, a great deal of it extremely valuable, some of it potentially destructive to faith. Especially in recent years, doubt seems almost to be celebrated and in some quarters is considered a prerequisite to faith, a stepping-stone to strong belief. One problem with believing and teaching such a thing is that some members of the Church who have never had noticeable periods or seasons of doubt just might suppose that (1) their faith must not be as strong and stable as that of persons who labored painfully with doubt; or (2) they ought to seek out or welcome doubts into their lives to complete the supposed faith formula. Both ideas are false and potentially hazardous. Neither encouraging doubt nor glorying in it is spiritually healthy or wise. President Harold B. Lee remarked that "it has been said by some who speak loosely that 'he who never doubted, never thought.' [We] must understand that faith, not doubt, is the beginning of all learning, whether in science or religion."⁵

"Intelligent people cannot long endure . . . doubt," Elder John A. Widtsoe stated. "It must be resolved. . . . We set about to remove doubt by gathering information and making tests concerning the subject in question. . . .

"*Doubt, therefore, can be and should be only a temporary condition.* Certainly a question cannot forever be suspended between heaven and earth; it is either answered or unanswered. As the results of an inquiry appear, doubt must flee. . . .

"The strong man is not afraid to say, 'I do not know'; the weak man simpers and answers, 'I doubt.' *Doubt, unless transmuted into inquiry, has no value or worth in the world.* Of itself it has never lifted a brick, driven a nail, or turned a furrow. To take pride in being a doubter, without earnestly seeking to remove the doubt, is to reveal shallowness of thought and purpose."⁶

In a devotional address to Brigham Young University students, Elder Marcus B. Nash of the Seventy pointed out that "each of us comes into this world with weakness, which I will define as desires or tendencies inconsistent with the plan of salvation. Such things, to one degree or another, are inherent in the human condition." He also observed that because Satan is aware of the great power that comes through faith in God's plan, "he seeks to weaken and ultimately destroy it. Time has shown that among the most effective weapons in his war against faith are sin, fear, and doubt." He noted that many members of the Church "conflate the idea of questions with the concept of doubt. *Questions and doubt are not the same thing.* We can seek answers to honest questions with doubt, or we can do so with faith. The choice is ours. . . . *Having faith means that we do not know all the answers to all the questions all the time, but we choose to live our lives consistent with the gospel truths we do know because we trust our God!* So heed not the mocking and often condescending voices of those who have lost faith."

Elder Nash declared that "the Lord's command to 'doubt not, fear not' (D&C 6:36) is akin to King Benjamin's instruction to '[put] off the natural man' (Mosiah 3:19). . . . *Doubt too can be a part of the natural man experience,* and it too will canker the soul if left unchecked." Elder Nash then added that rather than over-react or underreact when doubts creep in, "see doubt for what it is: a natural-man impulse that can paralyze your thinking and actions. Then exercise your faith in the Father and in the Son by patiently and diligently living the gospel and trusting that light and understanding will come to those who patiently seek learn-ing by study *and* by faith. It is beautifully, eternally productive to combine study and faith."[7]

Cyprian, a great defender of the faith after the apostolic pe-riod, remarked: "Into my heart, purified of all sin, there entered a light which came from on high, and then suddenly, and in a marvelous manner, *I saw certainty succeed doubt.*"[8]

But What If . . .

Now, having learned what the scriptures and latter-day Church leaders have taught concerning doubt, let's take a few moments to have a reality check. Doubt exists. Among Latter-day Saints. Among Saints who do in fact have testimonies of the restored gospel. I can still remember how I felt when I first read the following words from the preface of Elder Bruce R. McConkie's masterwork, *The Promised Messiah*: "I was born with a testimony, and from my earliest days have known with absolute certainty of the truth and divinity of his great latter-day work. Doubt and uncertainty have been as foreign to me as the gibber-ish of alien tongues."[9] I was deeply touched by his words, and I sensed then that Elder McConkie was an honest man, that he meant exactly what he said.

My next thought was, "Boy, wouldn't that be nice!" Why? Because I had faced doubts directly on a number of occasions, had struggled to come to faith, had wrestled with questions for which there did not then seem to be available answers. Further, I have known many remarkable and godly people who also had gone through seasons of unrest, times of spiritual drought, periods when divine responses to petitions seemed just out of reach. Mother Teresa of Calcutta is a prime example of one who, in spite of nearly half a century of yearning to feel divine approbation and love, pleading for the closeness to Deity that all believers crave, and yet having those desires unfulfilled, kept on. She kept going, until the day she died. Day in and day out, she charitably and humbly went into the streets to greet and feed and lift and love the "poorest of the poor," to offer tenderness, affection, and healing.[10]

No one should feel ashamed or less worthy when doubts arise. Like questions, doubts seem to be a part of our probationary estate. I agree with Latter-day Saint historian Patrick Q. Mason when he wrote: "Stigmatizing doubt to the point that people feel guilty for even having questions is not conducive to spiritual growth. Neither is it helpful to ignore questions as if they are invalid, unimportant, and wrongheaded. After having spent time in the scholarly trenches with many if not all of the issues that typically trouble people, and as one who has had countless conversations with those who feel their faith is teetering on the edge, I can strongly assert that the challenges are real and that most of the people who face them are earnest."[11]

For some, doubts take the form of "I'm not so sure that I really believe living that particular principle is spiritually worthwhile," or "I'm having difficulty reconciling my feelings of love and respect for our Church's leaders with the position the Church took on . . ." or "Can't I believe the Book of Mormon contains beautiful and uplifting teachings and marvelous precepts without believing it is a record of an actual pre-Columbian people?" or "Would it really complicate things in the Church if women were ordained to the priesthood?"

These are examples of matters about which some Latter-day Saints wrestle. And some of those are beloved, even lifelong, friends of mine. They are serious concerns to our brothers and sisters, and they should be taken seriously by those who desire to provide answers and strengthen their faith. Elder M. Russell Ballard explained to teachers in the Church Educational System, "Gone are the days when a student asked an honest question and a teacher responded, 'Don't worry about it.' Gone are the days when a student raised a sincere concern and a teacher bore his or her testimony as a response intended to avoid the issue. Gone are the days when students are protected from people who attacked the Church."[12]

There have been times when I allowed a question here and there in my life to morph into a doubt, when a doctrinal or historical issue took an extended period to understand or resolve. But one of the most profoundly moving and even startling of my moments of doubt came several years ago while I was simply sitting in our living room. My wife, Shauna, was away at the time, and I had spent a few hours reading. One of our daughters was going through a difficult illness. For some reason, I found myself worrying and fretting in what I now acknowledge was disproportionate to the situation at the time. She was quite sick, but there was nothing to suggest that her condition was life threatening. And yet I found myself thinking the worst—what would happen to her husband and children, how would he would get by, and how would their children survive without their mom.

But that was not the deepest anguish nor the most poignant fear. I found myself reflecting deeply during the next fifteen minutes on such dark questions as, What if there is no life after death? What if this life is all there is? What if, when we die, we simply cease to exist? What if we would never see our daughter again after we laid her in the grave? The situation was entirely new to me because I had never in my life entertained such doubts. The pain, the sorrow, the gloom and bitterness, the darkness that shrouded my soul are almost impossible to describe now; all I can say is that for a period of time I found myself where I had never been before: in a mood of absolute existential despair, drowning in doubt and consumed by the pain of eternal separation. I wept and shuddered, shook my head and cried out, "No, no! It can't be!"

And then, as quickly as those evil and empty and distressing thoughts had entered my mind, they left. The Spirit of God rested upon me, and I felt that reassuring peace that passes all understanding: the tender assurance that God lives and that he is in his heavens; that the plan of salvation is in very deed the great plan of happiness; that Jesus has in truth burst the bands of death and led captivity captive; that his rise from the tomb signaled and certified that we, too, will rise from the grave in glory; and that life and love and learning are forever. In short, my soul was reassured and rested in the knowledge that all that I had been taught, all that I had read and studied, all that I myself had taught in various venues in different parts of the world, was true. It was true! Oh, the unspeakable relief I felt! It was as though the lights had been switched on and the darkness dispelled. Like Lamoni, I was keenly aware and attuned to the fact that the "dark veil of unbelief [had been] cast away from [my] mind, and the light which did light up [my] mind . . . was the light of the glory of

God." Indeed, that "light had infused such joy into [my] soul, the cloud of darkness having been dispelled" (Alma 19:6).

As I sat pondering on what had just taken place, my mind and heart were overrun with a mixture of thoughts and feelings: I poured out my heart in gratitude to my Heavenly Father for the spiritual study in contrast I had just experienced. I thanked God for the testimony of Jesus that had been planted in my heart some six decades before. I praised him for allowing me to sense, for a brief moment, just how gloomy and helpless so many of earth's inhabitants feel when a loved one departs this life or when they themselves look into the eyes of the grim reaper. Consequently, I grieved for a time with all those in the world who sorrow in the face of death without hope of deliverance and the firm knowledge of the immortality of the soul. Even now as I contemplate that sobering experience, I am overwhelmed with feelings of appreciation and love for the Father and the Son, for their care and tender mercies. My doubt, ugly and overwhelming as it was, had been dispelled by a far greater power.

Conclusion

Ours is a beautiful world, and it is spiritually healthy to rejoice frequently in the Lord and in the magnificence of his creations. Ours is also a troubled world. We live in what some of the prophets have called the Saturday evening of time, in the eleventh hour.[13] Three millennia before the coming of Jesus Christ to earth, Enoch the patriarch-prophet was shown (as were many of the Lord's seers) a panoramic vision of things past, present, and future. He saw that "the heavens shall be darkened, and a veil of darkness shall cover the earth; and the heavens shall shake, and also the earth; and great tribulations shall be among the children of men, *but my people will I preserve;* and righteousness will I send down out of heaven; and truth will I send forth out of the earth, to bear testimony of mine Only Begotten" (Moses 7:61–62; emphasis added).

That "veil of darkness" Enoch saw can take many forms. The irony is staggering when we consider that in our day millions upon millions of pieces of data and information can be retrieved in almost the snap of a finger, while at the same time we are witnessing "a famine in the land, not a famine of bread, nor a thirst for water, but of hearing the words of the Lord." Amos prophesied that "they shall wander from sea to sea, and from the north even to the east, they shall run to and fro to seek the word of the Lord, and shall not find it" (Amos 8:11–12).

The blessed word of the Lord, particularly that certitude and assurance that come from the member of the Godhead known as the Witness or Testator, can and will come to the honest in heart. Men and women, young and old, need not languish in doubt, nor need they wrestle forevermore with disturbing questions. Compounding doubt and spreading uncertainty need not characterize the Latter-day Saints, for there is a more excellent way; there is a brighter future. We can look at the world—and even look at our questions or doubts—through the "eye of faith" (Alma 5:15; 32:40; Ether 12:19). To do so is simply to be open, attentive, teachable, even flexible, for "the things of the Spirit are to be 'sought by faith'; they are not to be seen through slit-eyed skepticism."[14] We need not yield to despair or settle for second best when it comes to knowledge and understanding and conviction. We are not alone, for we have received the soothing and satisfying word of Jehovah: "My people will I preserve" (Moses 7:61). May we be open to the Master's gracious effort to preserve and protect us.

Chapter 4

HOW DID WE GET HERE?

Several times during the past decade I have turned to my wife, Shauna, and asked, "How did we get here?"

Not knowing what I might be thinking about, she has patiently asked, "What are you talking about?"

I have then inquired, "How did we get to the point in our world where the nuclear family is becoming more and more difficult to find? Where the number of marriages that end in divorce is about the same as the number that hold together? Where racial conflict, bigotry, senseless killing of the innocent, are everyday occurrences? Where violence, harshness, crudeness, and insensitivity are the order of the day? Where cheating and stealing and false witness and immorality are becoming the norm? Where many of our elected officials in government, in the name of party loyalty, have forsaken any semblance of civility, respect, and tolerance, to the extent that some of our nation's most severe challenges are going unattended? Where boys and girls, men and women, no longer demonstrate the simple courtesies that once graced our communities?

We live in the day of an information explosion, a time when data is being processed and disseminated far faster than we can incorporate or inculcate it or what it means. We also live in a time of moral erosion, indicating clearly that our decency has not kept pace with our discoveries. As a world, and more particularly as a nation, we have drifted from our moorings, strayed from the faith of our fathers and mothers. The world has, in the last half century, undergone massive, even cataclysmic change.

Our society today is the product of several worldviews that are competing with the Judeo-Christian perspective. When I wondered why my college students saw things so radically different from the way I do, I had to remind myself that in many ways they are the product of their times. When I grieve that my children do not seem to possess the same zeal and excitement about going to Church and participating in its activities, I need to remember that how they view the world has been colored greatly by a different way of perceiving reality. Let's consider some of the factors pressing upon the souls of young and old in the twenty-first century.

The Trivialization of Religion

In the early 1960s a strange and to some frightful sound was heard throughout the academic world of religious studies—the cry that "God is dead." Protestant, Roman Catholic, and even Jewish theologians spoke often of godless theologies, Christless Christs, and Christian atheism, phrases that at first blush seem meaningless and absurd. The essence of this rhetorical requiem was that God had died in the hearts of men and women, that "God [had] passed out of our existence and become a dead entity for us because we crowded him out of our consciousness in creating and worshipping idols of our own ethnic likenesses."[1] The Lord's preface to the Doctrine and Covenants characterizes our time: "They seek not the Lord to establish his righteousness, but every man walketh in his own way, and after the image of his own god, whose image is in the likeness of the world, and whose substance is that of an idol, which waxeth old and shall perish in Babylon, even Babylon the great, which shall fall" (D&C 1:16).

The "God is dead" movement, though not necessarily characteristic of the rank and file of the religious world (or even typical of the views or feelings of the average priest, minister, rabbi, or imam), nevertheless symbolized a growing dis-ease in society, a loss of confidence in religious life, and a gradual distancing from religious values and time-honored traditions. Though the spiritual pendulum would yet swing during the 1970s with the rise of the charismatic movement and Christian fundamentalism, yet the age of existential anguish, of moral malaise, of cynicism and skepticism and doubt would take its terrible toll.

In recent times, where religion has not been rejected outright, it has been either ignored or in many cases trivialized. As Yale professor of law Stephen L. Carter pointed out, "One sees a trend in our political and legal cultures toward treating religious beliefs as arbitrary and unimportant, a trend supported by a rhetoric that implies that there is something wrong with religious devotion. More and more, our culture seems to take the position that believing deeply in the tenets of one's faith represents a kind of mystical irrationality, something that thoughtful, public-spirited American citizens would do better to avoid." Professor Carter continued: "The consistent message of modern American society is that whenever the demands of one's religion conflict with what one has to do to get ahead, one is expected to ignore the religious demands and act . . . well . . . *rationally.*" He further observed that "one good way to end a conversation—or start an argument—is to tell a group of well-educated professionals that you hold a political position (preferably a controversial one, such as being against abortion or pornography) because it is required by your understanding of God's will. In the unlikely event that anyone hangs around to talk with you about it, the chances are that you will be challenged on the ground that you are intent on imposing your religious beliefs on other people. And in contemporary political and legal culture, nothing is worse."[2]

As Elder Neal A. Maxwell put it, "The adversary has done well in persuading many people that those who are religious are naïve, ineffectual, or insincere Elmer Gantry types along with promoting the deception that any authoritarian religious commitment automatically means a Jonestown."[3]

The Loss of a Moral Sense

Certain problems arise when people either deny or ignore absolute truths. Two religious writers have stated: "One of the prime reasons this generation is setting new records for dishonesty, disrespect, sexual promiscuity, violence, suicide, and other pathologies, is because they have lost their moral underpinnings; their foundational belief in morality and truth has been eroded. . . . At one time, our society, by and large, explained the universe, humanity, and the purpose of life from the Judeo-Christian tradition: a belief that truth existed, and everyone could know and understand it. A clear understanding of what was right and wrong gave society a moral standard by which to measure crime and punishment, business ethics, community values, character, and social conduct. . . .

"That has changed dramatically, however. Our children are being raised in a society that has largely rejected the notions of truth and morality, a society that has somewhere lost the ability to decide what is true and what is right. Truth has become a matter of taste; morality has been replaced by individual preference."[4]

In the 1960s a second movement began to take shape—hand in hand with the "God is dead" movement—that has had its flowering in our own time. It was known as situation ethics or ethical relativism. Inspired by the writings of Bishop John A. T.

Robinson and Professor Joseph Fletcher, this movement proposed that any moral system is too shallow to provide answers to all situations and that every man and woman must decide for themselves what is right. It was a time when all were told to open themselves to the "new morality." "The sanctions of Sinai have lost their terrors," Robinson observed, "and people no longer accept the authority of Jesus even as a great moral teacher. Robbed of its supranatural supports, men find it difficult to take seriously a code of living that confessedly depended on them."[5] Some persons in our society are old enough to recall from the 1960s how common it was to hear young people spout off with "It's all relative" or the even more common dictum, "There are no absolutes" (a pretty absolute statement, to be sure). In the twenty-first century the die is cast, and what was once parlor conversation or even quaint college conversation has become applied theology.

As Latter-day Saint Christians, we know from dispensations past the social trauma that comes about as people attempt to move the standards, shift the anchors, or dilute the doctrine (especially the "hard" doctrine) to enhance a public image. Indeed, if those called to be the salt of the earth—those who have come out of the world by covenant (D&C 101:39–40)—lose their savor, either by mixture or by contamination,[6] wherewith shall the world be salted or the people be saved?

Denying Personal Responsibility

The growth of the behavioral sciences in the last century and a half has been phenomenal. Society seems at least as eager to understand the behavior and motivation of humankind as to understand light waves and black holes and the mysteries of DNA. The application of scientific principles to the study of human behavior—in an effort to formalize and objectify that study—has too often resulted in the superimposition of a cause-effect model on humans. Though it may be healthy and in some cases helpful to search for root causes, the cause-effect, stimulus-response model for understanding humanity will forevermore yield deficient and perhaps even perverse results when we ignore the role of moral agency and individual responsibility in that process.

Our fascination with causes ancillary to human agency has led us to paint ourselves into a corner in today's world. "The moral relativism of the modern age," the late political scientist James Q. Wilson observed, "has probably contributed to the increase in crime rates, especially the increases that occur during prosperous times. It has done so by replacing the belief in personal responsibility with the notion of social causation and by supplying to those marginal persons at risk for crime a justification for doing what they might have done anyway."[7]

Add to this trend the attack our society has made on guilt—the inner monitor by which we sense within ourselves that we have violated the laws of God or the norms of society—and we find ourselves in a precarious position. "That kind of thinking," one Protestant minister observed, "has all but driven words like *sin, repentance, contrition, atonement,* and *redemption* out of public discourse. If no one is supposed to feel guilty, how could anyone be a sinner? Modern culture has the answer: people are *victims.* Victims are not responsible for what they do; they are casualties of what happens to them. So every human failing must be described in terms of how the perpetrator has been victimized."[8]

Now to be sure, there are real victims in society—abused children or spouses, persons who suffer on account of racism or sexism, for example—and they deserve our compassion, our support, and our zealous defense against such ugliness. My specific concern is with individuals who do wrong, who knowingly violate the laws of decency and morality, and then seek refuge behind the growing wall of victimization. Consider the following examples:

"A man who was shot and paralyzed while committing a burglary in New York recovered damages from the store owner who shot him. His attorney told a jury the man was first of all a victim of society, driven to crime by economic disadvantages. Now, the lawyer said, he is a victim of the insensitivity of the man who shot him. Because of that man's callous disregard of the thief's plight as a victim, the poor criminal will be confined to a wheelchair for the rest of his life. He deserves some redress. The jury agreed. The store owner paid a large settlement. Several months later, the same man, still in his wheelchair, was arrested while committing another armed robbery.

"Bernard McCummings parlayed a similar victimism into wealth. After mugging and brutally beating an elderly New York man in the subway, McCummings was shot while fleeing the scene. Permanently paralyzed, he sued and won $4.8 million in compensation from the New York Transit Authority. The man he mugged, a cancer patient, is still paying doctor bills. McCummings, the mugger—whom the courts deemed the greater victim—is now a multimillionaire."[9]

Absolute Truth

So what do we do in the midst of all of this? How are we to respond? We are children of an Almighty God, believers in the divinity and saving power of Jesus Christ. How are we to make our way—and point out that way to our children and grandchildren—in a world whose standards no longer parallel our own? First of all, let's begin with the certain assurance that we cannot solve spiritual maladies through temporal solutions. Our problem in the world today is a detachment from morality, and morality cannot, in the long run, be severed from religion. Religion ties us back to God and to sacred things. To define morality in terms of utility (what works) or in terms of consensus (what most people believe) is to fall short of what was, is, and is to be (D&C 93:24).

Some things are. They just are. Neither judicial decisions nor popular opinion changes absolute truth. "Truth never changes," President Charles W. Penrose, then a member of the Quorum of the Twelve, taught more than a century ago. "Our conception of a truth may change as we grow in wisdom and understanding, and in clearness of spiritual vision. That which appeared to us to be true at one time we may find out later to be incorrect, and so it is we who change, and not the truth that changes."[10]

"We know instinctively that some things are right and some things are wrong. Let [a young woman] discover, for example, that her soccer shoes were stolen from her school locker and she'll feel wronged. She would not argue that the thief is entitled to his opinion of right and wrong; she would appeal to an objective sense of justice because she would claim that she had suffered an injustice. In so doing, of course, she would appeal to a moral law that she believes everyone—not just herself—ought to follow." That is to say, while many who speak of ethical relativism or situational ethics do so from their philosophical perch above the real world, those same persons expect others to treat them according to a model of truth and morality that reflects a more objective and absolute way of knowing what is right or wrong. If it is true that "there are no atheists in foxholes," then it is also true that "there are no relativists who expect to be treated relatively."[11]

The poignant message of the Savior is that happiness, meaning lasting joy, comes only to those who are built upon his gospel and whose works are really the Lord's works. So many people, as C. S. Lewis observed, seek to "invent some sort of happiness for themselves outside God, apart from God. And out of that hopeless attempt has come nearly all that we call human history—money, poverty, ambition, war, prostitution, classes, slavery—the long terrible story of man trying to find something other than God which will make him happy. . . . *God cannot give us a happiness and peace apart from Himself,* because it is not there. There is no such thing."[12]

In addressing himself to the growing relativism in the land, Elder Neal A. Maxwell pointed out that "there is a large difference between choosing to lie, and saying there is no real truth to be served anyway. There is a stark difference between hypocrisy, with its tacit admission of standards, and, on the other hand, saying there are really no standards to be violated." Those "who wrongly and heedlessly do their own thing are really doing Lucifer's thing in an unconscious pattern of sobering servility."[13]

Precept, Principle, Person

Let me propose what might be a rather typical discussion between a Latter-day Saint father and his child:

Father: "Billy, is it wrong to steal?"

Son: "Yeah, Dad, it's wrong to steal."

Father: "Why is it wrong?"

Son: "Because you taught us that it's wrong."

Father: "That's right, son, we did. But why did we teach you that?"

Son: "Because the Church teaches us that it's wrong to steal."

Father: "Right again. But why does the Church teach that?"

Son: "I guess because the scriptures teach us it's wrong to steal."

Father: "They do indeed. But let me ask you this: Why do you think the scriptures teach us that stealing is wrong?"

(Long pause.)

Son: "I don't know, Dad. Is it because Heavenly Father doesn't want us to steal?"

Father: "You're absolutely right, Billy. Heavenly Father does not want us to steal. Why doesn't he want us to steal?"

(Longer and even more uncomfortable pause.)

Son: "I don't really know, Dad."

This fictional encounter highlights a problem we face in teaching one another (and especially our children) the principles of morality and decency. Notice that the PRECEPT of "Thou shalt not steal" is pretty clear in this young man's mind. He has been taught the commandments and is able to articulate what he understands. A little less clear is that which underlies the precept, namely the PRINCIPLE, in this case the principle of honesty. Our young man knows what has been forbidden (to steal), and he senses that the main reason it is forbidden is that his parents, his Church, his scriptures, and his Heavenly Father have forbidden it.

Now those are all fine sources for the precept and the principle, but are they the ultimate, or absolute, source? No, for beneath the principle is the PERSON of God. A vital part of the great plan of happiness is the nature and kind of Being we worship. Fundamental to the purpose of life and the hope for glory hereafter is the knowledge that has been revealed concerning God—his character, his perfections, his relationship to us, and, most important to this discussion, the knowledge that we can become as he is.

To complete our conversation—

Father: "Billy, we are commanded not to steal [the Precept] because the Lord wants his people to be honest [the Principle]. He wants us to be honest because he is a God of truth [the Person]. He wants us to be holy because he is holy. We are sent to earth to strive as best we can to become as he is. Only as we become a person of truth can we ever hope to be like our Heavenly Father."

It is one thing to teach that honesty is the best policy (utility) or to teach that it is best to be honest because most people in society expect us to deal respectfully and responsibly with one an-other (consensus). Both utility and consensus have done much in the past to maintain some semblance of order in our world. With changing times and the erosion of time-honored values, however, many look about hopelessly for a more solid and enduring foun-dation. That foundation is doctrinal; it is the foundation of faith and revealed truth. Our children deserve answers to the hard question of WHY. And the only lasting and satisfying answer to why we do what we do or why we do not do other things is to be found in the great plan of happiness, in the understanding of God and humankind, in the clear statement of our eternal possibilities here and hereafter.

While serving as a priesthood leader, I had occasion to listen to wonderful young people confess serious moral transgressions. I asked about why the violation of the law of chastity is so serious and listened attentively as they spoke of disappointing their par-ents, postponing temple marriage or missions, having children out of wedlock, and contracting deadly diseases—all of which are substantial reasons to stay morally clean. But there is more to it, much more, and it is that added light and added knowledge that come from our divinely given doctrine to which we turn for the greatest preventative medicine against serious sin.[14]

Look to the Doctrine

President Boyd K. Packer emphasized a particular Book of Mormon passage again and again: "God gave unto them com-mandments, *after having made known unto them the plan of re-demption*" (Alma 12:32; emphasis added). From a knowledge of the person of God, as well as the doctrines and principles that follow, come the precepts. President Packer explained to Church Educational System personnel: "Young people wonder 'why?'—Why are we commanded *to do* some things, and why are we commanded *not* to do other things? A knowledge of the plan of happiness, even in outline form, can give young minds a 'why.' . . .

"Providing your students [or, we might add, our children, grandchildren, even other ward or branch members] with a collection of unrelated truths will hurt as much as it helps. Provide a basic feeling for the whole plan, even with just a few details, and it will help them ever so much more. Let them know what it's all about, then they will have the 'why.' . . .

"You will not be with your students or your own children at the time of their temptations. At those dangerous moments they must depend on their own resources. If they can locate themselves within the framework of the gospel plan, they will be immensely strengthened.

"The plan is worthy of repetition over and over again. Then the purpose of life, the reality of the Redeemer, and the reason for the commandments will stay with them.

"Their gospel study, their life experiences, will add to an evergrowing witness of the Christ, of [his] Atonement, of the restoration of the gospel."[15]

In short, as President Packer had said some years before, "True doctrine, understood, changes attitudes and behavior."[16]

Having said all this, I hasten to add that even with a knowledge of the great plan of happiness before them, individuals may choose to walk in the ways of the world and thus settle for less than they could have enjoyed. Nonetheless, I am convinced that the proper teaching of the Father's plan will do much to strengthen those who are children of the covenant and heirs to the promises made to Abraham, Isaac, and Jacob.

After the Storm

As we look about us today, we see influences, philosophies, and worldviews that, when adopted, can disconnect the children of God from God, influences that entice, attract, and persuade young and old to trade the eternal for the evanescent, or temporary.

Consider the following:

1. The growing *secularization* of our society. Something is secular when it pertains "to worldly things or to things that are not regarded as religious, spiritual, or sacred; temporal."[17] Thus when we speak of the secularization of our society, we are referring to the gradual shifting of religion and spiritual matters from the center to the periphery, until they are eventually pushed out of the picture completely. As Professor Wilson pointed out, religious persons or religious matters have not just been ignored but marginalized. Any attempt in the public square to speak of moral values or of what is right or proper is spurned as an effort to foist one's religious beliefs on others.

Whereas a hundred years ago religion was central to the outlook of most adults, we have in recent decades become prey to a growing secularism, a worldview that seeks to make sense of life without reference to God or the divine. If there is no real purpose to life, no God, no system of salvation, no hope of a life beyond the grave, and no divine parameters by which to distinguish right from wrong—in short, if anything goes, then eventually everything goes.

Possibly the most significant thinker to describe secularism is Charles Taylor, professor emeritus of philosophy at McGill University. In his monumental work, *A Secular Age*, Taylor described three phases or intellectual stages through which the Western world has passed to bring us to where we are now. First, there was once a time when it was impossible *not* to believe. There was simply no other way to explain things—the earth, the cosmos, nature, etc. Second came an acceptance that perhaps it is *possible* not to believe. The eighteenth-century Enlightenment, or Age of Reason, opened the door to that possibility. And third, in the case of many who speak of themselves as intellectuals, it has gradually become *impossible to believe*.

If we consider where we were in the first stage and then compare it to where we are today in the third stage, it is not difficult to recognize, sadly and solemnly, that we have undergone a complete 180-degree shift. As Christian scholar Albert Mohler pointed out: "Now there are not only alternatives to the biblical worldview available, but these alternatives are declared to be superior. Indeed if nonbelief was an oddity in the first stage—so much that it was considered eccentric and even dangerous—in this third stage it is theism [a belief in God] that is considered eccentric and dangerous." Why? Because "people who believe in God are dangerous people who do dangerous things. They are a deadly toxin within the culture at large."[18] A modern apostle, Elder Neal A. Maxwell, observed keenly that "the reactions to the Restoration cross a spectrum from rage to rejoicing. Little wonder that it is so, because the Restoration so profoundly affects our views of God, self, others, life, and even the universe. Given the pervasive secularization of society, the Restoration came none too soon."[19]

2. The rise of *militant atheism*. Atheism, or a belief that there is no God, has been with us for a long time. The word *atheism* did not appear in the English language until 1568, when it was used by Miles Coverdale. Within recent decades, however, a new breed of atheist has been spawned—angry, loud, attacking, and assertive unbelievers who work tenaciously to proselyte others to their way of thinking. "The New Atheists are, in their own way, evangelistic in intent and ambitious in hope. They see atheism as the only plausible worldview for our times, and they see belief in God as downright dangerous—an artifact of the past that we can no longer

afford to tolerate, much less encourage. . . . They have added new (and very important) arguments to the atheistic arsenal. . . . They know that the most important audience is the young, and they are in a position to reach young people with their arguments."[20] While their numbers in the United States may be relatively small, their voice is loud and their influence surprisingly broad.

3. A growing *discontent with traditional religion* and religious organizations. The 1960s assault on "the establishment" by university students has broadened and deepened in this century to include assault on *religious organizations*. Millions have voted with their feet, simply walking away from the church, the synagogue, the mosque, and the faith of Mom and Dad. This is not simply a passing fad, a youthful phase to treat lightly, for we are speaking of a stunning number of persons in our nation (some estimates run as high as 20 to 25% of the population). When these persons are asked about their religious persuasion, they answer "none." When they are polled about their feelings concerning religion or church, they respond that they are "done" and explain that they march to a different drummer and do their "own thing." Consequently, this unaffiliated group is often referred to as the "nones" and the "dones." A familiar refrain from them is that they are "spiritual but not religious."

A study by the Public Religion Research Institute suggests a slightly different rationale for persons forsaking their religious tradition. "A majority of the religiously unaffiliated—the so-called nones—say they fell away from faith not because of any negative experience, but because they 'stopped believing,' usually before the age of 30. . . . And while one-third of all nones say they do not believe in God, only 13 percent accept the label 'atheist.'"[21]

This withdrawal from faith is reflected even more markedly in the larger society. Sociologist Christian Smith at Notre Dame has classified many of the younger generation of our day as "moralistic therapeutic deists." According to Smith, the following beliefs basically describe their "religious" perspective:

- There is a God who created the world and set things in order. He cares about earth's inhabitants and watches over us.
- The Almighty wants everyone to be nice, to be kind and fair to others. This is what the Bible teaches.
- The whole purpose behind our lives is to be happy and to feel good about ourselves.
- God did create the world, but when he did, he established laws that could guide and govern all things. Hence God does not need to be especially involved in the details of our lives except when we have a problem to solve.
- If we live a good life and are a good person, we will go to heaven when we die.[22]

Smith and his coresearcher labeled the young people as *moralistic* because of their "Christianity lite" approach to life—be a good person, and you'll be fine. Such concepts as sin, repentance, forgiveness, and the need for prayer are almost completely lacking in their worldview. They may also be called *therapeutic* because they seem to view God as the grand problem solver, the cosmic therapist, the divine figure whose purpose is to keep people happy. They may be labeled as *deists* because their view of God's involvement (or lack of involvement) in the world parallels to some extent the view of the eighteenth-century Christian Deists who believed in what many have called the "watchmaker God," a being who created all things, set the laws in motion—wound up the clock, as it were—and let things run their course.

4. A generalized *relaxation of standards and levels of commitment*. This attitude manifests itself in numerous ways: a

disheveled lifestyle, irreverence, sloppy dress, loose and often vulgar language, indifference, and an attitude of "whatever." In addition, as members of the Church, young and old, absorb and identify with the values of our favorite stars of Hollywood and TV sitcoms, we allow the spiritual and moral desensitization to chip away at our own house of faith. When such practices as social drinking, cohabitation, the constant use of profane and vulgar expressions, violence, and the denigration of the nuclear family and traditional marriage—when such practices are paraded before us day in and day out, we gradually become desensitized and decrease the distance between ourselves and the values of the world.

Conclusion

To be sure, most Latter-day Saints hold to the rod of righteousness and stand boldly in defense of absolute truths and God-given standards of goodness and decency. There are, however, enough who have slipped from participating in the Church (in truth, one is enough) for us to think seriously about "how we got here." Some major currents of thought seem to be acting upon the minds of young and old, worldviews that are foreign to the Father's great plan of happiness, at odds with the teachings and practices of the everlasting gospel of Jesus Christ. We have moral and ethical challenges in our day that earlier generations did not face. While just knowing the source doesn't necessarily solve the problem, it may help. We must first know our enemy before we can prepare to do battle with it.

And yet while there are difficulties and dangers on all sides of us, while many of today's distraught parents wring their hands anxiously because of the society into which their children and grandchildren are entering, we may take comfort in the truth that "they that be with us are more than they that be with them" (2 Kings 6:16). God has not sent us here in this day and age to fail. He has not reserved some of his best and brightest for a time like this so that they might yield themselves to satanic influences or foreign perspectives on life. Looking down through the stream of time, Nephi, son of Lehi, beheld in vision "that the great mother of abominations did gather together multitudes upon the face of all the earth, among all the nations of the Gentiles, to fight against the Lamb of God. And it came to pass that I, Nephi, beheld *the power of the Lamb of God*, that it *descended upon the saints of the church of the Lamb, and upon the covenant people of the Lord*, who were scattered upon all the face of the earth; *and they were armed with righteousness and with the power of God in great glory*" (1 Nephi 14:13–14; emphasis added).

There will never again be an apostasy of the Church of Jesus Christ. God has called seers, noble men who see "things . . . not visible to the natural eye" (Moses 6:36), things down the road and sometimes around the corner. These are chosen men whose hearts are single to the divine glory, they are watchmen on the tower whose apostolic gifts enable them to give to us that elevated perspective, that enhanced vision that will see us through troubled times such as our own. They deliver "the word of God, which is quick and powerful, which shall divide asunder all the cunning and the snares and the wiles of the devil, and lead the man [or woman] of Christ in a strait and narrow course across that everlasting gulf of misery which is prepared to engulf the wicked—and land [our] souls, yea, [our] immortal souls, at the right hand of God in the kingdom of heaven, to sit down with Abraham, and Isaac, and with Jacob, and with all our holy fathers, to go no more out" (Helaman 3:29–30). We need not fear nor take counsel from fear. Let us be spiritually poised to receive the prophetic word and be valiant in following that counsel. Therein is our safety. Therein is peace.

Chapter 5

WHY PEOPLE LEAVE

There are perhaps as many reasons why individuals choose to leave The Church of Jesus Christ of Latter-day Saints as there are individuals who leave. Someone I know who has chosen to leave the Church wrote: "There is no smoking gun—no one thing that pushes people out of the Church." But some do leave, and by "leave the Church" I refer to (1) those who formally request that their names be removed from the records of the Church; (2) those who through the action of a disciplinary council are severed from the Church; and (3) those who drift from activity.

President Dieter F. Uchtdorf explained that "the search for truth has led millions of people to The Church of Jesus Christ of Latter-day Saints. However, there are some who leave the Church they once loved.

"One might ask, 'If the gospel is so wonderful, why would anyone leave?'

"Sometimes we assume it is because they have been offended or lazy or sinful. Actually, it is not that simple. In fact, there is not just one reason that applies to the variety of situations. Some of our dear members struggle for years with the question whether they should separate themselves from the Church.

"In this Church that honors personal agency so strongly, that was restored by a young man who asked questions and sought answers, we respect those who honestly search for truth. It may break our hearts when their journey takes them away from the Church we love and the truth we have found, but we honor their right to worship Almighty God according to the dictates of their own conscience, just as we claim that privilege for ourselves."[1]

During the years I served as a bishop and then as a stake president and also, for four decades, as a religious educator, I observed the following as some of the reasons why individuals choose to leave:

1. *They were not fellowshipped properly.* Almost always the full-time missionaries do their job well—they teach investigators the principles of the gospel, baptize the people, and deliver the new converts into the hands of members in the local branch or ward. Too often, though, that is the point where the proverbial ball is dropped—the members and priesthood leaders do not rush in, do all they can to maintain the convert's enthusiasm for the gospel, introduce them to their new Church family, and socialize them properly.

President Gordon B. Hinckley taught: "Having found and baptized a new convert, we have the challenge of fellowshipping him and strengthening his testimony of the truth of this work. We cannot have him walking in the front door and out the back. Joining the Church is a very serious thing. Each convert takes upon himself or herself the name of Christ with an implied prom-ise to keep His commandments. But coming into the Church can be a perilous experience. Unless there are warm and strong hands to greet the convert, unless there is an outreach of love and concern, he will begin to wonder about the step he has taken. Unless there are friendly hands and welcome hearts to greet him and lead him along the way, he may drop by the side." President Hinckley summarized the matter like this: "There is absolutely no point in doing missionary work unless we hold on to the fruits of that effort. The two must be inseparable." Drawing upon Moroni 6:4, President Hinckley taught that every new convert is entitled to three things: a friend; an assignment or Church calling; and nourishing by the good word of God.[2]

Unfortunately, some members who become troubled by doctrinal or historical matters are marginalized by believers, whether consciously or unconsciously. At a crisis point in their lives, when they most need love and attention and time, sometimes they are treated as though they are radioactive. One member of the Church very close to me commented that as she began attending "post-Mormon" meetings, she first noticed how friendly the members of this new group were to her. She described them as "nice, normal, respectable people just trying to do the right thing and standing up for what they believed. . . . I . . . felt more fellowshipped in this community than I ever did at church." That is tragic. Surely we can do better than that.

2. *They do not feel that they fit in.* Sometimes those who are unmarried do not feel a part of their ward because of the strong emphasis on families. As one friend who stopped coming to Church painfully expressed it, "I'm sure that the leaders of the Church agonize over what to do for the exponentially growing number of single members, but as a whole the Church has no place for single people. . . . As a single person in the Church, it is physically, emotionally, and spiritually excruciating to be alone, and it is in your face at all times." Some married couples who have not yet had children or who are unable to do so often do not feel a part of their ward. Occasionally brothers and sisters who find their social or political views different from those of their congregation wonder whether they can ever be accepted for who and what they are. Some whose testimony is weak, whose conviction of the faith is quite small, may feel overwhelmed in a

testimony meeting by the powerful and solid testimonies of other members who speak with certitude.

One of the most significant spiritual gifts that a member of the Church of Jesus Christ can possess is the gift to perceive or sense when a friend or acquaintance or ward member is in need, is hurting, needs a friend right now. That help may come in a smile, a kind greeting, in moving from your accustomed place in the chapel to sit with this person. Small acts of kindness and sensitivity can go a long way in securing and solidifying another member of the Church. The small effort to reach out is more than compensated for by the potentially eternal rewards.

3. *They don't want to be members any longer.* Some persons who have just come into the Church, and even some who have been a part of the Church for many years, suddenly or gradually make the difficult decision to leave the Church for any number of reasons: they simply don't want to attend three hours of Church meetings on Sunday, pay tithing and other offerings, live the Word of Wisdom, serve as a visiting or home teacher, and so forth. They are not bad people, not rebellious, and they may have no unkind feelings toward anyone or anything in the Church. They may well appreciate all that they have learned, all within the Church who have meant so much to them, or what the Church stands for. They just want to discontinue affiliation.

Some, of course, no longer believe in the restored gospel. One acquaintance explained: "When I talk about leaving the Church, I don't mean those people who stop going for this or that reason and yet still believe. I'm talking about people who leave because they feel it is untrue. It is heartbreaking and offensive when members of the Church claim that we were offended, or we are too lazy to fulfill our callings, or that we don't care enough. Those statements are deeply troubling because most of those I know who leave do so after intense study and thoughtful and prayerful attempts at making it work." This person commented on a label that is often attached to one who leaves: "The term *anti-Mormon* is also incredibly offensive, as it creates the same feeling as the term *anti-Semite*. I am not an anti-Mormon, and although the Church caused a great deal of pain for me, its people are also my people. It is my culture and the only religious tradition I know. Leaving the Church was like losing a limb, and although I have considered removing my name from the records, I have not done so and most likely will not."

We wish, obviously, that everyone would choose to stay, but, as President Uchtdorf pointed out, we believe in individuals' moral agency, their right to determine how their life will be spent, what they will do and not do, who or what they will worship. Parting may prove painful, and so we as members of The Church of Jesus Christ of Latter-day Saints should strive to be as sympathetic and loving as we can. The last thing in the world such persons need—and I suggest that the Lord would definitely not want this—is for members of his Church to turn their backs on those who were once their Church friends, to spurn or shun them in any way. Such painful situations call for true Christians to manifest genuine kindness and thoughtful understanding.

4. *They have unresolved doctrinal or historical issues.* The Internet has proven to be a phenomenal blessing to the world and to members of the Church. It is almost inconceivable how quickly one can acquire information on myriads of subjects in no time at all. The Internet has also, however, proven to be a challenge to us, because everything from strictly orthodox Latter-day Saint teachings to subtle or even blatant, vicious attacks on the faith may be found there. And to complicate matters, obviously not all of what is available is true or accurate. But it's in writing, and, sadly, that's all some folks need to assume that what they are reading is the way things really are and really were. In some cases

what is available is true, but the author's interpretation of the teaching or event may lack context or the requisite background for correct understanding.

When I have counseled with members of the Church who were deeply troubled by such matters as Brigham Young's statements on Adam-God, the Mountain Meadows Massacre, the priesthood restriction, origins of the book of Abraham, or other areas of concern, I have often asked questions such as the following:

- Did you ever have a testimony of the truthfulness of the restored gospel?

- When did you first begin to sense that this work was true?

- Can you describe the occasion? What did it feel like? What thoughts accompanied the feelings you had at the time?

- What convinced you, for example, that the Book of Mormon was in fact another testament of Jesus Christ, a true scriptural record?

- How much of a factor in your spiritual conviction was your intellect?

- What part of your overall testimony was solely dependent on facts and propositions?

- When did you begin to feel that perhaps the restored gospel was not true? What led to that conclusion?

- Have you earnestly prayed about this matter? Has God revealed to you, by the power of the Holy Spirit, that all that you previously believed is not true?

- Where it applies, are you now persuaded that your marriage in the temple is meaningless and that you are not really sealed for eternity to your spouse and children? What will be the effect of that decision on your family?

- To what extent has your recent period of questioning and doubt required you to go back in time and reinterpret your past, reinterpret what you once felt and thought?
- Are you now prepared to conclude that the numerous occasions on which you felt the promptings and guidance of the Spirit, the ratifying approval of God upon a sermon, a testimony, or a priesthood ordinance were not genuine?

This kind of exercise is essentially a guided tour back through the past to the time when the person I was speaking with had received a testimony of the truthfulness of the restored gospel. Such an endeavor may well be an example of what President Uchtdorf described as "doubting your doubts" in his October 2013 general conference address. When something as serious as the eternal welfare of a soul is at stake, we must make certain that a decision of the magnitude required to leave the Church receives at least the same care and attention that the initial quest to know the truth required.

Am I suggesting that the questioner ignore troublesome issues or pretend that supposed contradictions do not exist? No, not at all. I am proposing, however, that to attend only to one's rational processes, to make monumental decisions of the soul on the basis alone of one's intellect—what we think we now understand—is at best unwise and at worst spiritually perilous. Early in this dispensation, the Saints were instructed by revelation to "give heed unto all his [Joseph Smith's] words and commandments which he shall give unto you as he receiveth them, walking in all holiness before me; for his word ye shall receive, as if from mine own mouth, *in all patience and faith*" (D&C 21:4–5; emphasis added).

There's the key: We are to receive—and, I suggest, evaluate—the Prophet's words, and, for that matter, the whole of the Restoration, *in patience and faith*. We should be *patient,* because sometimes the answer, the clarification, the solution to the problem, may not come for a while. We are to receive the Prophet's words *in faith* in the sense that there are some things that cannot be known through the five physical senses, matters of deep import that can, as Paul said, be known only by the power of the Spirit of God (1 Corinthians 2:11–14)—that is, by a meta-physical sense, a sense above and beyond what the grandest and most complex of scientific instruments can measure or assess. When it comes to spiritual matters, often *the heart begins to reveal things to the mind that it did not know.* Very often, believing is see-ing. As Alma taught, "Faith is not to have a perfect knowledge of things; therefore if ye have faith ye hope for things which are not seen, which are true" (Alma 32:21).

5. *They are troubled because they are learning some things for the first time.* Other troubled Latter-day Saints indicate that many of the sensitive issues that have arisen, particularly those that in-volve the history of the Church, caught them totally by surprise because they had never heard such things before. Some even accuse the Church of covering them up. As historian Patrick Mason put it, "One of the primary reasons why some members of the church have become disenchanted, disappointed, or even angry in recent years is because they were never taught to ex-pect skeletons in the closet of church history and so are shocked when they find them. . . . A person could conceivably attend a lifetime of three-hour Sunday blocks and never hear about the Mountain Meadows Massacre or discrepancies in Joseph Smith's accounts of the first vision." Mason pointed out that Church leaders, in an effort to inspire and edify the members, have often chosen to present the best possible image of the Church, both to those within and those outside our faith. It is not a matter of secret cover-ups but rather "an act of ministry." He suggested that "those who are disappointed that church meetings are not

as intellectually stimulating or historically nuanced as university classes suffer from category confusion; they would surely not expect or appreciate a sermon from their college professor." Further, "the church is primarily concerned with preaching the gospel of Christ, not adult history education. . . . Much of our church literature and teaching, especially on Sundays, is devoted to a presentation of the gospel able to reach the widest spectrum of church membership. This is not only appropriate but beautiful and redemptive."[3]

Keep in mind that the Restoration is an unfolding drama, that light and knowledge, understanding and perspective, are coming to the Saints gradually, precept upon precept. This is not just the case with doctrinal understanding; it holds for our history, as well. Latter-day Saint historian Keith A. Erekson pointed out that "important pieces of the Church's history have not yet been discovered. . . . In the study of history, [however,] the absence of evidence is not a valid cause for doubt. Learning about the past is an effort of gathering as much trusted and, where possible, verifiable evidence while reserving final judgment on the portions of history that we are unable to fully understand because of the lack of information."[4] The Church's intensified effort in recent decades to uncover and catalog historical documents and details and make them available to members of the Church as well as to persons of other faiths—is a gradual process. We learn bit by bit, item by item, historical event upon historical event. We understand much more now about our history, especially during the ministry of the Prophet Joseph Smith, than we knew when I was a student at Brigham Young University. Much of this discovery has come as an outgrowth of the remarkable Joseph Smith Papers Project. For example, I remember that in one of my very first religion classes at BYU, a Church history class, my professor, Paul Cheesman, referred to an account of the First

Vision (the earliest, 1832, account) that he himself had recently discovered as a result of his research. Many details concerning the translation of the Book of Mormon have come to light in recent years as historians have carefully sifted through materials of which we were, for the most part, ignorant.

Several years ago a ward Relief Society president mentioned to me that in a Relief Society lesson the instructor had quoted from the journal of one of her ancestors. The ancestor had been present in early August 1844 in Nauvoo when Brigham Young was transfigured before the Saints and took on the appearance and voice of Joseph Smith. Another woman in the class remarked quickly that the sisters ought not put too much stock in that particular testimony, since there were so few accounts of the purported event.

The president asked me what I knew about that historical moment, and I explained that I was aware of many accounts of that incident. I did some checking with people who know much more about our history than I do and discovered that in recent years scores of accounts of that miraculous experience had been found in pioneer journals.[5] The woman who spoke up may have done so in all good faith, supposing that accounts she had read or heard about the transfiguration of Brigham Young were few and far between. In the meantime, however, many, many descriptions of that experience had come to light. In short, there are many things we know now that we did not know until recently. We are learning as we go.

6. *They are troubled by the fallibility of Church leaders.* As Latter-day Saints, we love the scriptures and thank God regularly for them. We believe, however, that one can have sufficient confidence and even reverence for holy writ without believing that every word between Genesis 1:1 and Revelation 22:21 is a word-for-word dictation of the Almighty or that the Bible now

reads as it has always read. Indeed, our own scriptures attest that plain and precious truths and many covenants of the Lord were taken away or kept back from the Bible before it was compiled (1 Nephi 13:20–29; Moses 1:40–41; Articles of Faith 1:8).[6] We still cherish the Holy Bible, recognize and teach the doctrines of salvation within it, and seek to pattern our lives according to its timeless teachings.

In like manner, we can sustain with all our hearts the prophets and apostles without believing that they are perfect or that everything they say and do is exactly what God wants said and done. In short, we do not believe in apostolic or prophetic infallibility. As we have been reminded again and again, whom God calls, God qualifies. That is, God calls his prophets. He empowers and strengthens the individual, provides an eternal perspective, loosens his tongue, and enables him to make known divine truth. Being called as an apostle or even as president of the Church, however, does not make him perfect. President David O. McKay, then a member of the Quorum of the Twelve Apostles, explained that "when God makes the prophet He does not unmake the man."[7] A more recent apostle, Elder D. Todd Christofferson, reminded us that "not every statement made by a Church leader, past or present, necessarily constitutes doctrine. It is commonly understood in the Church that a statement made by one leader on a single occasion often represents a personal, though well-considered, opinion, not meant to be official or binding for the whole Church. The Prophet Joseph Smith taught that 'a prophet [is] a prophet only when he [is] acting as such.'"[8]

Prophets are men called of God to serve as covenant spokesmen for his children on earth, and thus we should never take lightly what they say. The early Brethren of this dispensation were the living prophets for their contemporaries, and much of what we believe and practice today rests on the doctrinal foundation they laid. The work of the Restoration, however, entails a gradual unfolding of divine truth in a line-upon-line fashion. Some years ago my late colleague Joseph Fielding McConkie said to a group of religious educators: "We have the scholarship of the early brethren to build upon; we have the advantage of additional history; we have inched our way up the mountain of our destiny and now stand in a position to see things with greater clarity than did they. . . . We live in finer houses than did our pioneer forefathers, but this does not argue that we are better or that our rewards will be greater. In like manner our understanding of gospel principles should be better housed, and we should constantly be seeking to make it so. There is no honor in our reading by oil lamps when we have been granted better light."[9] Ultimately the Lord will hold us responsible for the teachings, direction, and focus provided by the living oracles of our own day, both in their commentary on canonized scripture as well as in the living scripture that is delivered through them by the power of the Holy Ghost (D&C 68:3–4).

"From our perspective today," Brother Erekson wisely observed, "we obviously know more than participants did about the outcome of the past, *but we also know far less about their experience of living in it. The people who lived in the past belonged to their own times and places and circumstances.* To have charity for their differences and empathy for their experiences, we must begin with humility about our own limitations. *It requires humility not to judge people in the past by our standards.* It requires humility to admit we do not know everything, to wait patiently for more answers, and to continue learning."[10]

In reminding the Saints of Lehi's teaching relative to "opposition in all things" (2 Nephi 2:11), Elder Dallin H. Oaks observed that some of the opposition the Church faces "comes from Church members. Some who use personal reasoning or wisdom to resist prophetic direction give themselves a label borrowed from elected bodies—'the loyal opposition.' However appropriate for a democracy, there is no warrant for this concept in the government of God's kingdom, where questions are honored but opposition is not (see Matthew 26:24).

"As another example," Elder Oaks pointed out, "there are many things in our early Church history, such as what Joseph Smith did or did not do in every circumstance, that some use as a basis for opposition. To all I say, exercise faith and put reliance on the Savior's teaching that we should 'know them by their fruits' (Matthew 7:16)."[11]

7. *They do not feel they are enjoying the intellectual stimulation or the private spiritual experiences that ought to be had by members of the Church of Jesus Christ.* In recent years I have encountered a number of members of the Church, as well as former members of the Church, whose chief criticism is, "I don't get anything out of Church any more," or "I go to Church hungry and come home unfed. It's the same old stuff over and over."

As a religious educator myself, I am especially attentive to such complaints. Too often teachers in the Church do not take the time to prepare properly; they come to their classes and attempt to wing it, that is, teach without preparation, talent, or substance. Others called to teach do not prepare well and depend on God's assistance to enable them to teach by the Spirit. That is foolish. The Holy Ghost bears testimony of truths that are taught, of doctrines that are set forth, of propositions that are delivered. There is no such thing as teaching by the Spirit when there is no substance to the lesson or sermon. The Holy Spirit must have something about which to certify and confirm. We could clearly do better to make our lessons more interesting, more relevant, more meaningful. Having the fulness of the gospel is no excuse for presenting it poorly.

Having said that, let me hasten to add that what we experience in our worship services or in our lessons is largely a matter
of our individual expectations and our individual participation.
First, a word about *expectations*. What is it I expect to happen
in a sermon or a lesson? Is it realistic to suppose that the speaker
or teacher will consistently bring forth new doctrinal insights or
formerly undiscovered historical details? Not really. Is it reasonable to suppose that we will spend most of our time in Church
dealing with the "meat" of the gospel of Jesus Christ? Not really.
Why? In a church like ours, Brother and Sister Johnson, who
joined the Church forty years ago, are frequently in the same
chapel and in the same classroom with Brother and Sister Taylor,
who were baptized Saturday. Because of that, because of the di-
versity of experience and understanding within a given ward or
branch, it will probably be the case that in Church meetings we
will consistently teach the "milk" of the gospel, the fundamental
principles and doctrines. Such teachings will stretch the Taylors,
will motivate them to read and search and pray and seek for clarity and for deeper understanding. The acquiring of "meat," the
obtaining of deeper and more profound insight, is largely an individual responsibility.

And what about the Johnsons? How do they attend class and
not be bored to tears or frustrated by hearing things they have
heard a hundred times? Now we turn to a consideration of *participation*. What might the Johnsons do to derive the most spiritual
benefit from class? They could partake of a few ounces of humility and not suppose they know everything that is to be known.
They could read the scriptural passages (or other lesson material) assigned for that day's lesson, study them carefully, and come
prepared to make a contribution in class. That contribution may
take the form of listening intently, thinking seriously, and seeking for divine guidance in finding new meaning, new applications

for the scriptural passages or prophetic statements. It may take the form of making a few worthwhile comments and observations throughout the lesson. It may take the form of praying earnestly for the instructor that she or he will be guided, empowered, and inspired in teaching the truth and leading the class discussion. No matter how much we know, no matter how much formal education we have, no matter how many scholarly works we have devoured, there is always room to learn and experience more at Church. But it will usually require humility and openness on our part. Elder Neal A. Maxwell wrote that "meekness is needed not alone to open to us understandings but also to keep us free and intellectually active. Meekness with its emerging spiritual resilience also provides a soft landing for hard doctrines."[12]

In recent years there has grown up in our midst, especially in what we might call the heartland of the Church, an attitude and mindset that manifest a serious case of spiritual impatience. These members of the Church, presumably dissatisfied with the elementary manner in which a study of the gospel is undertaken, have chosen to turn toward more flashy, more sensational, certainly more dramatic means of gaining great knowledge and having unusual experiences. I call this group the "Mormon Gnostics," some of whom may be characterized by (1) their enthusiasm, almost obsession, for the esoteric, for "deeper" matters of the faith; (2) their claim to be enjoying what might be called extraordinary spiritual experiences—regular visits from the Savior himself or consistent conversations with such notable prophets as Enoch or Melchizedek; (3) their eagerness to discover and broadcast precisely when the Lord Jesus Christ will return in glory. When it comes to matters that ought wisely to be left with the prophets and apostles, the Savior is very emphatic that "it shall not be given to any one to go forth to preach my gospel, or to build up my church, except he be ordained by some one who has authority, and *it is known to the church that he has authority and has been regularly ordained by the heads of the church*" (D&C 42:11; emphasis added).

"You cannot force spiritual things," President Boyd K. Packer explained. "Such words as *compel, coerce, constrain, pressure, demand* do not describe our privileges with the Spirit.

"You can no more force the Spirit to respond than you can force a bean to sprout, or an egg to hatch before its time. You can create a climate to foster growth; you can nourish, and protect; but you cannot force or compel. You must await the growth.

"Do not be impatient to gain great spiritual knowledge. Let it grow, help it grow; but do not force it, or you will open the way to be misled."[13]

8. *They find themselves at odds with the Church's leadership on social or moral issues.* It has been half a century since I entered the Mission Home in Salt Lake City to begin my formal preparation for full-time missionary service. After a glorious week of testimonies and instruction from members of the First Presidency, Quorum of the Twelve Apostles, and First Council of the Seventy, our group of about three hundred left for various missions. As I recall, there were then about thirteen thousand full-time missionaries throughout the world. After arriving in New York City (the headquarters of the Eastern States Mission), I was assigned to work for a short time in Manhattan and then transferred to Greenfield, Massachusetts. I remember well what it felt like to look into the eyes of total strangers and bear testimony of a message of great importance—that God had chosen to reestablish his Church on the earth and had called modern prophets to lead and provide divine guidance for that Church. In most cases, the people were thoroughly uninterested in what we had to say, but occasionally we would stumble across a genuine truth seeker willing to consider our message.

While my companion and I were knocking on doors in a small town in Massachusetts, a lovely woman, probably in her mid-forties, came to the door, opened it, and with a smiling face asked what she could do to help us. I was bold enough to reply that actually we had come to do something for her.

"Oh," she said, "that's good news. So what can you do for me?"

I responded eagerly, "We have come to bring a message to you that God is indeed our Heavenly Father, that he loves every one of his children, and that he has chosen to bless us by sending modern prophets into the world."

She stood a little straighter and said, "Modern prophets? What do you mean?"

I spoke briefly of the boy Joseph Smith's search for the truth, his desire to know which of all the churches in his village he should join, and his glorious experience in the Sacred Grove. One of the reasons I remember this particular conversation is I recall the feeling that came over me as I bore witness of the prophetic call of Joseph Smith. I was almost overcome with emotion, and as I looked deeply into the woman's eyes, I saw that she had been touched by the power of that same Spirit and knew in her heart of hearts that what I had just said was true. She asked us to say more, and my companion told of the coming of Moroni, the translation of a book of ancient American scripture, and of heavenly messengers sent to restore the authority to act in God's name.

Now she had tears in her eyes. She looked squarely at me and said, "I believe you are telling me the truth." She put her hand on her heart and said simply, "I feel it." She then explained that she would love to invite us in to tell her more, but that her husband would soon be home from work, and she was afraid he would not be interested in what we had to say. Then this sweet lady said, essentially, "I really do want to hear more; I hope my husband will feel the same way."

We set a time to return later in the week and then left. Sadly, when we did return, she greeted us at the door, apologized that her husband refused to allow us into the home, and then said tenderly, "I hope I will be able to learn more about your unusual message some day."

We left, heartbroken. I grieved for several days, because it was obvious that our testimony of modern prophets had struck a chord within her soul. I took some consolation in the knowledge that God is merciful and kind and that everyone will have an adequate and appropriate opportunity to hear the message of the Restoration, whether in this life or in the next. That particular incident and hundreds of similar ones in the next two years, combined with the priceless privilege of teaching and bearing witness of the restored gospel to tens of thousands of students at Brigham Young University, *convinces* me that there is a mighty power associated with the message of modern revelation and continuing prophetic direction.

That is our distinctive message to the world. It is a pearl of great price. I am moved by the Lord's instruction to Joseph Smith given in March of 1833: "Verily I say unto you, the keys of this kingdom shall never be taken from you, while thou art in the world, neither in the world to come; nevertheless, through you shall the oracles [revelations, divine direction] be given to another, yea, even unto the church." And now comes the clincher, a sobering directive, a type of warning: "And all they who receive the oracles of God, *let them beware how they hold them lest they are accounted as a light thing, and are brought under condemnation thereby,* and stumble and fall when the storms descend, and the winds blow, and the rains descend, and beat upon their house" (D&C 90:3–5; emphasis added). My sober assessment is that mighty storms are now beating upon us, horrific winds and rain are now pounding us with gale force, beating upon our house of faith.

In what was clearly a prophetic warning, Elder Neal A. Maxwell declared to BYU students: "Make no mistake about it, brothers and sisters; in the months and years ahead, *events will require of each member that he or she decide whether or not he or she will follow the First Presidency.* Members will find it more difficult to halt [hesitate, stumble, falter] longer between two opinions. . . . In short, brothers and sisters, *not being ashamed of the gospel of Jesus Christ includes not being ashamed of the prophets of Jesus Christ.*"[14]

If we have chosen to be baptized into The Church of Jesus Christ of Latter-day Saints, if we have taken upon us the covenants and ordinances associated with Church membership, if we once rejoiced and delighted in being a part of an organization that is led by prophets, seers, and revelators, are we still excited about it today? To wrest Alma's words from their context, if we once felt to sing gratitude and shout praises to the Almighty for sending modern prophets to the earth, do we feel so now? (see Alma 5:26). And if not, why not? Here are a few points to ponder:

- To what extent is there an exemption clause in our loyalty to the prophets?
- Where do we draw the line between following and not following the counsel and decisions of the prophets and apostles of the Church?
- Do we seek to know and then to follow prophetic direction, unless that direction conflicts with our own social, political, or moral views?
- Do the First Presidency and Quorum of the Twelve Apostles cease, in our eyes, to be living prophets when what they counsel is contrary to what we feel or have decided about a given issue?
- As Elder Maxwell inquired, "Do I believe in the living prophet even when he speaks on matters affecting me and

my specialty directly? Or do I stop sustaining the prophet when his words fall in my territory? If the latter, the prophet is without honor in *our* country!"[15]

- Do I believe the Brethren are true prophets when they deliver stirring and inspiring messages at general conference, when they write moving and motivational books, when they establish the Humanitarian Fund and offer the resources of the Church to needy persons of other faiths throughout the world, when they announce the Perpetual Education Fund, when they encourage members to be actively involved in Christian service in helping to calm the fears and meet the needs of homeless refugees, but not when what they declare to be the mind of God on matters pertaining to marriage and the family is at odds with society's values?

President Henry B. Eyring explained that "looking for the path to safety in the counsel of prophets makes sense to those with strong faith. When a prophet speaks, those with little faith may think that they hear only a wise man giving good advice. Then if his counsel seems comfortable and reasonable, squaring with what they want to do, they take it. If it does not, they consider it either faulty advice or they see their circumstances as justifying their being an exception to the counsel. Those without faith may think that they hear only men seeking to exert influence for some selfish motive."

Further, some erroneously suppose that "to take counsel from the servants of God is to surrender God-given rights of independence. But the argument . . . misrepresents reality. When we reject the counsel which comes from God, we do not choose to be independent of outside influence. *We choose another influence. . . .*

"Another fallacy is to believe that the choice to accept or

not accept the counsel of prophets is no more than deciding whether to accept good advice and gain its benefits or to stay where we are. But *the choice not to take prophetic counsel changes the very ground upon which we stand. It becomes more dangerous.* The failure to take prophetic counsel lessens our power to take inspired counsel in the future. The best time to have decided to help Noah build the ark was the first time he asked. Each time he asked after that, each failure to respond would have lessened sensitivity to the Spirit. And so each time his request would have seemed more foolish, until the rain came. And then it was too late."[16]

A colleague of mine, Professor Shon Hopkin, suggested another very sound, practical question for our consideration: Do I really want to be a part of a Church that agrees with me on every point? I would add: Is that my criterion for deciding what institution, what religious organization, I will associate with?

Matters pertaining to marriage, home, family, and sexual orientation have been in the news and in the courts for much of the past few decades. These tender topics are not just conversational matters about which curious observers may comment in disinterested fashion. No, they are real and poignant, because in many cases it is a member of our own or our extended family—or a beloved friend and associate—who is seeking love, support, and understanding. How we interact with spouses, children, or acquaintances who deal with same-sex attraction every hour of every day strikes at the heart of what it means to be a Christian, a follower of the Lord Jesus Christ. There is no place in the Church of Jesus Christ for hatred, bigotry, vicious speech, or even thoughtless insensitivity, for such feelings and actions are alien to the Spirit of Him who is the Prince of Peace, the Great Physician. As covenant people, we are called upon "to bear one another's burdens, that they may be light; yea, and . . . to mourn with those that mourn; yea, and comfort those that stand in need of comfort" (Mosiah 18:8–9). It is what Jesus himself would do; hence, it is what we are charged to do.

And yet, while loved ones are to be as caring and supportive as possible, there is no need to spurn or rebel against the Church's moral standard or even to contend for it to be altered, adjusted, or tweaked so that it will be in harmony with the current consensus in our world. As we have discussed, there are absolute truths, God-ordained values and virtues, that must be observed and upheld if society and the family unit are to be preserved. A mother or father, a brother or sister, a friend or associate need not choose between the Church of Jesus Christ and a loved one. Again, it is so very tragic, so terribly unnecessary, for members to choose to leave or disaffiliate from the Church or to slip into the ranks of the less active because of our leaders' counsel to maintain the Church's moral standard. President Thomas S. Monson observed, "Where once the standards of the Church and the standards of society were mostly compatible, now there is a wide chasm between us, and it's growing ever wider."[17] The simple plea of that same prophet is profound and extremely pertinent: "May we *maintain the courage to defy the consensus*. May we ever choose the harder right instead of the easier wrong."[18]

Through the years it has been my sweet privilege to become acquainted with some of those we sustain as prophets, seers, and revelators. They are ordinary men with an extraordinary calling, a weighty responsibility. Scripture teaches that seers are those who are watchmen on the tower (see Ezekiel 3:17; D&C 101:45), those who behold also "things which [are] not visible to the natural eye" (Moses 6:36), things "afar off" (D&C 101:54). "When the Spirit teaches prophets the truth of things as they really are," Elder Maxwell observed, "this includes sensitizing these special men to *the implications of what is just beginning,* implications that are imperceptible to others. Prophets are *alerted to tiny trends that bode ill for mankind*. Prophets, therefore, are *the Lord's early-warning system*: they both detect and decry at his direction. What may seem to be a premature expression of prophetic concern is actually the early discovery of a difficulty that will later plague the people."[19]

9. *One's personal behavior has slipped below gospel standards.* I have saved for last this reason why some persons have chosen to discontinue membership or association with the Latter-day Saints. I hasten to add that *this is not why most people leave.* But it is one reason. Some doubt because they are living in unrepented sin. As a priesthood leader, I once sat opposite a member of the Church who had just moved into our ward. He came in to see me to ask to have his name removed from the records of the Church. I asked him why. He responded, "Well, there are some serious doctrinal problems with Mormonism."

"Like what?" I followed up. "

Oh," he said, "there are some pretty deep theological issues that I simply cannot reconcile, and I'm not sure you are in a position to know much about them."

I replied, "Why don't we try one or two issues to see if I can't help just a bit." I pushed and persisted to get him to volunteer one of the "deep theological issues," but he continued to put me off. Within an hour it was clear what the real problem was—not intellectual but spiritual, for he had lived in wanton immorality for years. He didn't have questions about the doctrines of The Church of Jesus Christ of Latter-day Saints but rather about his own ability to abide by the standards of that Church. "Some have behavioral lapses," Elder Maxwell affirmed, "and then seek to cover these by pretending to have reservations about a doctrine or a leader. Having misbehaved, they try to cover their sins."[20]

Christian theologian Alister McGrath wrote: "In part, doubt

reflects the continued presence and power of sin within us, reminding us of our need for grace and preventing us from becoming complacent about our relationship with God. We are all sinners, and we all suffer from doubt, to a greater or lesser extent. . . . Sin causes us to challenge the promises of God, to mistrust him. . . . Our limitations as God's fallen and fallible creatures prevent us from seeing things as clearly as we would like." Sin prevents us from discerning "the big picture of the workings of God in the world."[21] Isn't that an apt description of Laman and Lemuel's state? They "did murmur because they knew not the dealings of that God who had created them" (1 Nephi 2:12).

As we have said, this final reason for leaving is probably not the reason of most persons who choose to disengage from The Church of Jesus Christ of Latter-day Saints. Experience teaches me, however, that occasionally a member's inappropriate conduct can in fact lead him or her to respond to what psychologists call "cognitive dissonance." If a woman is a heavy smoker and finds herself reading a newspaper article on how continued use of tobacco products may result in lung cancer, she may choose one of two courses to deal with her problem: (1) she can begin the difficult but rewarding process of overcoming the smoking habit, or (2) she can choose to stop reading the newspaper!

One who is under gospel covenant to keep the commandments of God and abide by the standards of the Lord's restored Church may slip into serious sin and, like our smoker, find that he is faced with a number of options: (1) he can face up to his misconduct and begin the difficult but rewarding path of repentance; (2) he can decide that he no longer believes the message of the restored gospel; (3) he can choose to leave the Church; and, in some cases, (4) he can allow his troubled conscience to canker his soul and cause him to begin to deny and defy the faith he once cherished.

Conclusion

The reasons why men and women determine to leave the Church of Jesus Christ and go elsewhere are as varied as the problems and the personalities of the people themselves. Obviously we wish they would choose to stay with us, to remain a part of the great work that will grow and spread to all parts of the earth. We wish we could say something or do something that would soothe troubled hearts, provide satisfying answers to difficult questions, persuade them to place their burdens or doubts on the shelf and keep searching for acceptable solutions *within* the household of faith. But of course every man and woman is free to choose their path in this life and select which guides they will and will not follow.

President Dieter F. Uchtdorf extended a tender invitation: "To those who have separated themselves from the Church, I say, my dear friends, there is yet a place for you here. Come and add your talents, gifts, and energies to ours. We will all become better as a result.

"Some might ask, 'But what about my doubts?'

"It's natural to have questions. . . . Therefore, my dear brothers and sisters—my dear friends—please, first doubt your doubts before you doubt your faith. We must never allow doubt to hold us prisoner and keep us from the divine love, peace, and gifts that come through faith in the Lord Jesus Christ. . . .

"If you seek truth, meaning, and a way to transform faith into action; if you are looking for a place of belonging: Come, join with us!

"If you have left the faith you once embraced: Come back again. Join with us!

"If you are tempted to give up: Stay yet a little longer. There is room for you here. . . .

"Come, join with us! For here you will find what is precious beyond price."[22]

There really are proven ways to find answers to hard questions and confront troublesome issues, and in many cases resolution and return are a very real possibility. No one of us can know everything. Frankly, it would be impossible to identify a member of the Church whose areas of training, experience, and expertise cover every topic. There are, however, many talented, devoted, and knowledgeable Latter-day Saints who are eager and willing to share what they know and assist us to reconcile what we supposed were irreconcilable concerns. Many answers are available.

Solutions to problems may be found, but the most effective and productive path is always one of patience and faith. The resolution of most serious challenges to one's faith requires both time and trust. Thus, don't be in too much of a hurry to give up on *what you don't understand,* and don't minimize or neglect *what you do know and understand.* The promise is sure: if we are faithful in a few things, God will enlighten and empower us to be able to solve and resolve many things (see Matthew 25:21).

Chapter 6

WHAT FAITH IS NOT

I really do want to know: Whatever happened to faith? Whatever happened to our ability to be patient in receiving answers, in assuming the best about our Church, its leaders, our scriptures, and our doctrines? We touched upon this question to some extent when we spoke of the significant, even cataclysmic changes that have taken place in our world in the past half century. The changes about which we have spoken are not merely scientific or technological changes, although such developments certainly alter our way of life. They are perspective, worldview—lenses through which we interpret life, death, why we are here, divine intervention, and the miraculous.

I might have posed the question differently: What happens when faith begins to wane in the hearts of men and women, when basic metaphysical beliefs begin to erode among earth's inhabitants? I suppose the answer would be, You have a world like our world today! So what kind of a world do we live in, at least as pertaining to faith?

These Are Not Faith

One approach to deciding what faith is, and why it is becoming so scarce in our world, is to first explore what it is *not*.

• *Faith is not gullibility or falling for anything.* Faithless people are sometimes quite critical of those who possess what they do not. They assume that people who live their lives by faith are naïve, easily swayed, and simple-minded. That is not faith. A faithful person is a thinking being, one who can judge, assess, and reason, one who can distinguish clearly between good and evil, light and darkness, right and wrong. A faithful person does not fall prey to either the foolish or the perverse. Faith can be exercised only in that which is true. President N. Eldon Tanner explained that faith "will avail us nothing unless it is based on true principles. This is illustrated in a story I have told before about the meeting of the Indians with the Europeans when they first began their explorations in the New World. The Indians were amazed at the power and explosive qualities of gunpowder and asked many questions about how it was produced. Taking advantage of the ignorance of [these people] and seeing an opportunity to increase their wealth through deception, the Europeans told them it came from the seed of a plant. The Indians believed them and purchased some seed in exchange for gold. They carefully planted the seed and watched it grow, but of course they did not get any gunpowder. No matter how sincere one's belief may be in an error, it will not change the error into truth."[1]

• *Faith is neither weakness nor ignorance.* True faith is anything but weak. The early Brethren of this dispensation were, in fact, taught that faith is a principle of power, the same power by which God created the worlds. Further, "the principle of power which existed in the bosom of God, by which the worlds were framed, was faith; and . . . it is by reason of this principle of power existing in the Deity, that all created things exist."[2]

Nor is faith the opposite of knowledge. A certain level of knowledge and understanding is needed before an individual can exercise faith. The School of the Elders learned, for example, that in order to exercise faith in God unto life and salvation, a person must (1) believe there is a God; (2) have a correct understanding of the character, perfections, and attributes of that divine Being; and (3) possess an actual knowledge that the course in life that he or she is pursuing is according to the will of God.[3]

"Faith is the child of knowledge," Elder Bruce R. McConkie wrote. "It is reserved for those only who first have knowledge; there neither is nor can be any faith until there is knowledge. No one can have faith in a God of whom he knows nothing. Faith is founded on truth; it is the offspring of truth; it can never exist alone and apart from the truth."[4]

• *Faith is not blind.* In fact, those with faith are frequently able to see and discern things that a faithless person could never perceive. That is why some say believing is seeing, not the reverse. Nor are Latter-day Saints, who are presided over by prophets, seers, and revelators, expected to follow their leaders like blind sheep. President Harold B. Lee said, paraphrasing Brigham Young: "The greatest fear I have is that the people of this Church will accept what we say as the will of the Lord without first praying about it and getting the witness within their own hearts that what we say is the word of the Lord."[5] One of the great strengths of the Church is that there are millions of people throughout the world who exercise bold, intelligent obedience.

Adam and Eve were commanded to "offer the firstlings of their flocks, for an offering unto the Lord. And Adam was obedient unto the commandments of the Lord." The Mosaic account indicates that "after many days" an angel appeared to our first father and inquired as to why he was making an animal sacrifice. His answer was beautiful: "I know not, save the Lord commanded me" (Moses 5:5–6). Was Adam obeying blindly? Not at all. Adam and Eve had already had a great deal of experience with the Almighty. The early Brethren of this dispensation learned that "after man was created, he was not left without intelligence or understanding, to wander in darkness and spend an existence in ignorance and doubt (on the great and important point which effected his happiness) as to the real fact by whom he was created, or unto whom he was amenable for his conduct. God conversed with him face to face. In his presence he was permitted to stand, and from his own mouth he was permitted to receive instruction. He heard his voice, walked before him and gazed upon his glory, while intelligence burst upon his understanding, and enabled him to give names to the vast assemblage of his Maker's works."[6] No blind obedience there.

• *Faith is not the absence of certitude.* I once heard one of my university students comment to a friend, "I don't enjoy listening to Elder _____ at general conference. He lacks humility."

His friend replied, "How do you know he is not humble?"

The response? "Listen to him carefully when he speaks. He is bold. He is confident. He is filled with certitude."

A strange assessment at best. Humility is the virtue of having a correct and accurate view of yourself, of knowing your strengths and your weaknesses. More important, it is knowing the source of your strength, the source of your power. President Gordon B. Hinckley declared: "Some time ago a journalist from a prominent national publication spoke in Salt Lake City. I did not hear him, but I read the newspaper reports of his remarks. He is quoted as having said, 'Certitude is the enemy of religion.' The words attributed to him have stirred within me much reflection. Certitude, which I define as complete and total assurance, is not the enemy of religion. It is of its very essence.

"Certitude is certainty. It is conviction. It is the power of faith that approaches knowledge—yes, that even becomes knowledge. It evokes enthusiasm, and there is no asset comparable to enthusiasm in overcoming opposition, prejudice, and indifference.

Great buildings were never constructed on uncertain founda-
tions. Great causes were never brought to success by vacillating
leaders. The gospel was never expounded to the convincing of
others without certainty. Faith, which is of the very essence of
personal conviction, has always been and always must be at the
root of religious practice and endeavor. . . .

"If the Latter-day Saints, as individuals, ever lose that certitude, the Church will dwindle as so many other churches have.
But I have no fear of that. I am confident that an ever-enlarging
membership will seek for and find that personal conviction which
we call testimony, which comes by the power of the Holy Ghost,
and which can weather the storms of adversity."[7] Indeed, faith
leads to and results in certitude.

• *Faith is not positive thinking, nor does it consist in willing something into existence.* Obviously it is a good thing to be positive, to
be upward looking, to be optimistic about now and the future.
One has to spend only a short time with a naysaying pessimist
to appreciate being with someone whose words are affirming, en-
riching, and edifying. And if any people in all the wide world
have reason to be positive, to rejoice frequently, it is the Latter-
day Saints. The gospel of Jesus Christ is the good news, the glad
tidings that Jesus of Nazareth was in very deed the Christ, the
Promised Messiah. It is celebratory news that through his atoning suffering in Gethsemane and on Golgotha, his death on the
cross, and his glorious rise from Joseph of Arimathea's tomb to
resurrected immortality, we may have our sins remitted, our souls
sanctified, our bodies and spirits reunited, never again to be divided, so as to receive a fulness of joy in the resurrection (D&C
93:33). Further, how could we possibly be negative and pessimis-
tic for very long, knowing that that same gospel has been restored
in our day in its fulness through the call of a latter-day prophet?
Because of the knowledge, power, covenants, and ordinances that

have been delivered to earth through God's legal administrators, we are enabled to "enjoy the words of eternal life in this world, and eternal life in the world to come" (Moses 6:59), including the continuation of the family unit into eternity.

But faith is not positive thinking. Nor can one with a positive attitude will things into being. Imagine a full-time missionary, a zone leader, serving, let's say, in France, who turns to the missionaries under his charge and says, "Come on, elders and sisters, if we just had the faith we could baptize this whole country!" The Gospel of Mark records that while in his hometown, Nazareth, the people heard the Savior's preaching and asked, "Is not this the carpenter, the son of Mary, the brother of James, and Joses, and of Juda, and Simon? and are not his sisters here with us? And they were offended at him. But Jesus said unto them, A prophet is not without honour, but in his own country, and among his own kin, and in his own house." Now note this astounding verse: "*And he could there do no mighty work*, save that he laid his hands upon a few sick folk, and healed them" (Mark 6:3–5; emphasis added). Now imagine that we heard someone standing fifty feet away from Jesus say, "Come on, Lord, just exercise your faith!" No, that would never be appropriate, not just because he is the Son of the living God, the second member of the Godhead. Jesus could not and did not reward faithlessness with a display of signs and wonders, because "faith cometh not by signs, but signs follow those that believe" (D&C 63:9).

The Book of Mormon records that approximately 350 years after the birth of Christ, Mormon sought earnestly to lead his wayward people back to faith. He had been appointed the leader of the Nephite armies and at about this time won a battle against the Lamanites. Mormon explained that "the Nephites began to repent of their iniquity, and began to cry even as had been prophesied by Samuel the prophet; for behold no man could keep that which was his own [see Helaman 13:37]. . . . Thus there began to be a mourning and a lamentation in all the land because of these things, and more especially among the people of Nephi." Mormon was thrilled, hoping against hope that something, anything, could bring about a conversion among his people. "But behold this my joy was vain, for their sorrowing was not unto repentance, because of the goodness of God; but it was rather the sorrowing of the damned, because the Lord would not always suffer them to take happiness in sin. And they did not come unto Jesus with broken hearts and contrite spirits, but they did curse God, and wish to die" (Mormon 2:10–14). Now picture some positive-minded, goal-driven, twenty-first-century person on the sidelines sounding off: "Mormon, Mormon. Come on, you've got to put your heart in it. Let's exercise some faith!"

In all three of these scenarios are factors over which the missionary, the Master himself, and the prophet-editor Mormon had no control. One of these factors—and a deeply significant one at that—is the moral agency of the people, their right to choose what they will do with their lives. Being positive and upbeat is great, indeed so much better than being deflated or living like Eeyore the donkey. But it is not faith.

• *Faith is not absolute certainty as a result of tangible, observable evidence.* Alma remarked in his marvelous discourse on faith: "Yea, there are many who do say: If thou wilt show unto us a sign from heaven, then we shall know of a surety; then we shall believe. Now I ask, is this faith? Behold, I say unto you, Nay; for if a man knoweth a thing he hath no cause to believe, for he knoweth it" (Alma 32:17–18). These verses are crucial to our understanding what it means to have faith in these latter days, a taxing time of spreading unbelief. Far too many people today— and some of these people are Latter-day Saints—want tangible, empirical, scientifically verifiable evidence for the truthfulness of the restored gospel. If we could demonstrate through DNA research that the Nephites and Lamanites were actual, pre-Columbian people and that the Lehite colony did in fact come from Jerusalem, then this critic will believe. If in the near future adequate and substantial archaeological evidences for the Book of Mormon peoples could be found, then the naysayer would be persuaded of the historicity of this Testament of Jesus Christ. If we could just prove convincingly that the eleven Egyptian papyri fragments held by the Church have something to do with Abraham the prophet, then that doubter will accept the book of Abraham as ancient holy scripture.

In using Thomas the apostle as an illustration, President Howard W. Hunter explained that "in a sense, Thomas represents the spirit of our age. He would not be satisfied with anything he could not see [John 20:19–29], even though he had been with the Master and knew his teachings concerning faith and doubt. . . . Faith does not take precedence over doubt when one must feel or see in order to believe.

"Thomas . . . wanted knowledge, not faith. Knowledge is related to the past because our experiences of the past are those things which give us knowledge, but faith is related to the future—to the unknown where we have not yet walked." President Hunter wisely observed: "Thomas had said, 'To see is to believe,' but Christ answered, 'To believe is to see.'"[8]

If we were to take Thomas's approach, we might well demand physical proof or a rational explanation for what Jesus did when he healed the lepers, the paralyzed, the woman with the issue of blood, blind Bartimaeus; when he multiplied the loaves and fishes and fed five thousand men; when he calmed the raging storm on the Sea of Galilee; when he raised from the dead the daughter of the Roman centurion, the son of the widow of Nain, and Lazarus, the brother of Mary and Martha. Can we provide scientific evidence for such miracles? No, we cannot. Then how do we know that they actually took place?

"All the scriptures, including the Book of Mormon, will remain in the realm of faith," Elder Maxwell taught. "Science will not be able to prove or disprove holy writ. However, enough plausible evidence will come forth to prevent scoffers from having a field day, but not enough to remove the requirement of faith. Believers must be patient during such unfolding."[9] In speaking of historical analysis, Latter-day Saint scholar Patrick Mason wrote, "There is nothing more unstable than basing one's life and outlook purely on the latest scholarship, let alone one's casual perusal of it. What appears to be solid is actually quite transient." In other words, "scholarship makes for a fairly wobbly foundation upon which to build one's profoundest commitments. I can't imagine a more maddening life than to rise each morning to consult the learned journals to see what one's position de jour is."[10]

Professor Hugh W. Nibley was a beloved twentieth-century Latter-day Saint apologist, a defender of the faith. I had the distinct pleasure, for a time, to serve as chair of his department at Brigham Young University, and I came to know something not only about his mind (which was amazing) but also a great deal about his soul. As many Saints know, he was a man of extraordinary intellect, but, perhaps more important, he was a disciple of the Lord Jesus Christ and a man of deep and abiding faith in the restored gospel. "The words of the prophets," he testified well over a half century ago, "cannot be held to the tentative and defective tests that men have devised for them. Science, philosophy, and common sense all have a right to their day in court. But *the last word does not lie with them.* Every time men in their wisdom have come forth with the last word, other words have promptly followed. *The last word is a testimony of the gospel that comes only by direct revelation. Our Father in heaven speaks it, and if it were in perfect agreement with the science of today, it would surely be out of line with the science of tomorrow.* Let us not, therefore, seek to hold God to the learned opinions of the moment when he speaks the language of eternity."[11]

• *Faith is not built on a weak foundation or on flimsy evidence.* I was asked some years ago by a mission president to speak to his missionaries at a zone conference. We had a healthy discussion and exchange of ideas. I was invited to stay for lunch and visit with the missionaries. I did a great deal of listening and learned much. One interesting conversation revolved around a young couple who were being taught by the missionaries but were not progressing. "They're golden people," one elder said, "ripe and ready for membership in the Church. They just won't commit to being baptized."

Several suggestions were made by the missionaries listening in—fasting with them, having the bishop meet with them, intensifying the friendshipping effort, etc., to all of which the first elder said, "We've tried that."

After a long pause, another elder inquired, "Have you given them the 'scrolls discussion'?"

The first elder responded, "No. Do you think this would be a good time for the 'scrolls discussion'?"

"Sounds like a perfect time to me," the first came back.

Now I had never heard of the "scrolls discussion." I was dying to know what it was, so I blurted out, "What's the 'scrolls discussion'?"

The second elder stared at me rather quizzically and said, "Surely, Brother Millet, you've heard of the 'scrolls discussion'?"

I indicated that I had not.

"The 'scrolls discussion,'" he said, "involves showing the people how the Dead Sea Scrolls prove the truthfulness of the Church!"

I replied, "Fascinating. How do they do that?"

"Well," he said, "as you know, the Dead Sea Scrolls contain information about a group of very early Christians out in the deserts of Judea."

I responded, "No, they don't. The Dead Sea Scrolls were written by a group of hyper-religious Jews."

He said, "Oh. I didn't know that." Then he said, "Well, you do know that they had three presiding high priests at the head of their church."

I indicated that the leaders of the group were Aaronic priests, not Melchizedek.

The elder went on. "Well, there's some fascinating doctrine within the scrolls that proves our doctrine to be true."

I commented that the scrolls were interesting historical documents, but they did very little for us doctrinally.

This exchange went on for about five minutes, the elder providing what he thought to be airtight "proofs" and I trying gently to let him know that most of what he understood about the Dead Sea Scrolls was simply untrue. I could see the frustration in his eyes. Finally he sighed and concluded, "Well, I'll just say this— the 'scrolls discussion' has always worked for me!"

I thought then (and since) about all the people who might have come into the Church as a result of what they learned in the famous "scrolls discussion." I shuddered.

Conclusion

Faith is NOT many things. We must be grounded and settled spiritually to exercise faith in the Lord Jesus Christ, faith in the power of redemption that comes only through the sufferings and death of Christ, faith in the Father's perfect plan of salvation, faith in the restored Church of Jesus Christ and its apostolic leadership. This is vital, for it is only a solid faith, an enduring and fruitful faith, that will empower us to "withstand the evil day" and to "quench all the fiery darts of the wicked" (D&C 27:15, 17). It is only through acting on a faith built on truth—"things as they are, and as they were, and as they are to come" (D&C 93:24)—that deep conversion takes place. Then we are able to face opposition calmly, encounter enemies kindly but boldly, and make our way through the mists of darkness to the tree of life.

Robert J. Matthews, former dean of religious education at Brigham Young University, counseled me on several occasions to be careful not to be found laboring in secondary causes. Elder Dallin H. Oaks declared that "the number of good things we can do far exceeds the time available to accomplish them. Some things are better than good, and these are the things that should command priority attention in our lives. . . .

"Some uses of individual and family time are better, and others are best. We have to forego some good things in order to choose others that are better or best because they develop faith in the Lord Jesus Christ and strengthen our families."[12]

The world has its counterfeits for faith. Consequently, one of the great needs of this dispensation is for the Saints of the Most High, those who have been called out of darkness into the Master's marvelous light (1 Peter 2:9), to obtain and exercise the gift of discernment—to discern truth from error, good from evil, that which is permanent from that which is transitory, that which is of greatest worth from that which is really of little consequence.

Chapter 7

WHAT FAITH IS

The increasing challenge each of us faces is to have and enjoy the benefits and blessings of faith in a day of relative unbelief. Few things are as desperately needed in our day as faith—faith in the unseen, faith in God's care, faith in the future, or as one astute observer of Christianity noted, "faith that bridges the chasm between what our minds can know and what our souls aspire after."[1] Faith is not whimpering acquiescence, not timid and spineless hope for happiness. Faith is active. Faith is powerful. Faith is based on evidence, the kind of evidence that men and women acquire who search and pray and open themselves to the Infinite, who refuse to yield to cynicism or arrogance.

Faith in Jesus Christ

Though we need not be simpleminded to have faith, we may need to be simple in our approach to life and its challenges in order to enjoy the fruits of faith. How open are we today to simple belief? Just how believing are we? How would we respond to miracles as in days gone by? The late Roman Catholic journalist Malcolm Muggeridge wrote: "In humanistic times like ours, a contemporary virgin—assuming there are any such—would regard a message from the Angel Gabriel that she might expect to give birth to a son to be called the Son of the Highest as ill-tidings of great sorrow and a slur on the local family-planning centre. It is, in point of fact, extremely improbable, under existing conditions, that Jesus would have been permitted to be born at all. Mary's pregnancy, in poor circumstances, and with the father unknown, would have been an obvious case for abortion; and her talk of having conceived as a result of the intervention of the Holy Ghost would have pointed to the need for psychiatric treatment, and made the case for terminating her pregnancy even stronger. Thus our generation, needing a Saviour more, perhaps, than any that has ever existed, would be too humane to allow one to be born; too enlightened to permit the Light of the World to shine in a darkness that grows ever more oppressive."

Muggeridge asked, "Are we, then, to suppose that our forebears who believed implicitly in the Virgin Birth were gullible fools, whereas we, who would no more believe such notions than we would that the world is flat, have put aside childish things and become mature? Is our skepticism one more manifestation of our having—in [Dietrich] Bonhoeffer's unhappy phrase—come of age?"[2]

What does it mean to have faith in the Savior? The epistle to the Hebrews contains perhaps the best-known definition: "Now faith is the substance [JST, "assurance"] of things hoped for, the evidence of things not seen" (Hebrews 11:1). Alma stated this truth slightly differently: "Faith is not to have a perfect knowledge of things; therefore if ye have faith ye hope for things which are not seen, which are true" (Alma 32:21). As followers of the Christ, we strive with all of our hearts to be worthy. Those who have tasted of the heavenly gift and enjoyed the sweet fruits of gospel living want more than anything to become, some day, some time, holy people. But we fall short. We make mistakes. We sin. And so we are not completely righteous. To put it another way, we are not, as a result of our own actions, just.

Theoretically, there are two ways a person could be just—meaning declared or esteemed innocent, guiltless, free from the demands of divine justice, to be in a proper standing, a proper relationship with God. First, he or she could live life perfectly, never taking a wrong step, never deviating one iota from the strait and narrow path. In such a case, it could be said of that person that he or she was *justified by law* or *by works*. It would be a glorious thing to be in such a state, would it not? The problem is that such a situation is purely hypothetical, for, except for Jesus, neither the greatest prophet nor the mightiest apostle has ever traveled life's paths without error or sin of some kind. It may be possible hypothetically, but it is impossible practically. That is what the prophets through the ages meant when they taught that "by the law no flesh is justified" (2 Nephi 2:5; compare Romans 3:20; Galatians 2:16).

The apostle Paul warned the Saints in his day about trying to establish their own righteousness, as the Jews had sought to do through their strict observance of the law of Moses: "Brethren, my heart's desire and prayer to God for Israel is, that they might be saved. For I bear them record that they have a zeal of God, but not according to knowledge. For they being ignorant of God's righteousness, and *going about to establish their own righteousness, have not submitted themselves unto the righteousness of God*. For Christ is the end of the law for righteousness to every one that believeth" (Romans 10:1–4; emphasis added). In the ultimate sense, as Jesus taught the lawyer, "There is none good but one, that is, God" (Matthew 19:17).

Paul put his own remarkable accomplishments and earthly attainments into perspective when he wrote: "I count all things but loss for the excellency of the knowledge of Christ Jesus my

Lord: for whom I have suffered the loss of all things, and do count them but dung, that I may win Christ, and be found in him, not having mine own righteousness, which is of the law, but that which is through the faith of Christ, the righteousness which is of God by faith" (Philippians 3:8–9).

This statement by Paul points toward the second way that we may become just—*by faith*. Faith is the total trust, complete confidence, and ready reliance upon the merits, mercy, and grace of Jesus Christ for salvation. It is a gift of the Spirit (1 Corinthians 12:9; Moroni 10:11), a divine endowment that affirms to the human heart the identity of the Savior and his redemptive mission. Though we might speak of faith in a broad sense as the underlying reason why people live and move and go about their daily activities, the principal and primary faith of which the scriptures speak is faith in the Lord Jesus Christ.

Because of the Fall, humanity is alienated from the Father and from things of righteousness; all are subject to spiritual death (Alma 12:16, 32; 42:9). No matter how noble their own efforts to overcome spiritual death, to love and serve others, or to keep the commandments of God, men and women will forevermore fall short of the divine standard. Their works, though acceptable to God, will always be insufficient to save them (2 Nephi 25:23). In short, had there been no means of bridging the chasm between sinful humankind and a sinless God, nothing that any human being could do would make up for the loss. Thus, there is a need for some means to reconcile finite mortals with the infinite Deity, to repair the breach between earth and the heavens. Because "all have sinned, and come short of the glory of God" (Romans 3:23), we cannot be justified by law or by works. Our only option is to be justified by faith, to turn to, confess, and trust in One who did in fact keep the law of God perfectly. It is only through the name of Jesus Christ—meaning his power or authority, his atoning mission and work—that salvation comes to the children of God (Acts 4:12; 2 Nephi 9:24; Mosiah 3:17; 26:22; Alma 22:13; Helaman 14:13). In the words of Amulek, the atonement of Christ "bringeth about means unto men that they may have faith unto repentance" (Alma 34:15).

In a day awash in cynicism and a time engulfed in doubt, to have faith in Jesus Christ is to believe that he was born of the virgin Mary; that from God the Father he inherited immortality, the capacity to live forever; that from Mary he inherited mortality, the capacity to die. To have faith in Jesus Christ is to believe that Jesus was fully human, that in coming to earth and assuming a physical body, the Almighty Jehovah, the God of Adam, Enoch, and Noah, came to know by personal experience just what it was like to experience disappointment, rejection, alienation, bitter irony, pain, and sorrow. Christ Jesus "humbled himself [literally, 'emptied himself'], and became obedient unto death, even the death of the cross" (Philippians 2:8). To have faith in Jesus Christ is simultaneously to believe that he was fully God, that there was no quality, no virtue, no divine characteristic missing from his nature. To have faith in Jesus Christ is to believe in his atoning sacrifice, that he "descended in suffering below that which man can suffer; or, in other words, suffered greater sufferings, and was exposed to more powerful contradictions than any man can be. But, notwithstanding all this, he kept the law of God, and remained without sin."[3]

To have faith in the Lord Jesus is to trust him. How so? How do we come to trust someone in this life? What does it mean to say that I trust my wife, Shauna? I trust her in that I know she loves me, that she knows me well enough to understand my heart, my deepest desires and longings. I trust her in that I know she knows, only too well, my weaknesses and my inclination to be less than I should be, and yet she displays the patience and long-suffering that is so often required on her part. I trust her because she is ever ready and willing to forgive me. I trust her in that I know I can share with her my heaviest burdens, my darkest moments, my lingering doubts, and know that she will think no less of me. Finally, I trust Shauna because I know that ours is a winning team, that our companionship blesses and elevates my life and makes me so much more, so much better, than I would be on my own. Further, I have confidence in her in that I know she will always come through. And heaven only knows how much I rely on her wisdom and judgment, her discernment, and her unending devotion and loyalty.

"Too often we construe faith in the Lord," Elder Neal A. Maxwell noted, "to mean only the acceptance of His existence, an acknowledgment that He is there. What is wanted, since He is there, is our *trust* in Him, *including His plans for us.* Let us not complain of large classes in this mortal school when, at the same time, we consistently decline His offers to tutor us privately."[4]

Faith in Christ's Church

As we have mentioned, we live in fascinating but scary times. Millions upon millions have walked away from organized religion, have declared themselves "nones" and "dones," have chosen to define themselves as "spiritual but not religious." Some suggest that rather than attend church, they can draw close to the Almighty in the mountains while paddling their canoe on a stream or lake and absorbing the beauty of nature. They are fully persuaded that spirituality is completely personal and has little or nothing to do with a religious organization. Don't get me wrong: I love the mountains, delight to be out on the river, and few things are more relaxing or therapeutic to me than returning to nature. And I am drawn to the need to deepen my communion with the Infinite. Too often, however, this state of mind presumes that we can make our way along the strait and narrow path on our own terms, supposedly by simplifying things, by taking the quick and easy route.

The fact of the matter is that we *need* the Church. Sister Bonnie L. Oscarson, Young Women General President, declared: "We believe that this Church is more than just a good place to go on Sundays and learn how to be a good person. It is more than just a lovely Christian social club where we can associate with people of good moral standing. It is not just a great set of ideas that parents can teach their children at home so they will be responsible, nice people. The Church of Jesus Christ of Latter-day Saints is infinitely more than all of these things."[5]

A lack of formal church organization eventually results in chaos, in individuals becoming their own priest and prophet, their own scriptural interpreter. We need the fellowship, since true Christianity is always lived out in community, in a body of believers who labor to establish Zion. We need the ordinances (the sacrament of the Lord's Supper, as well as the priesthood authority to baptize, confer the Holy Ghost, ordain, endow, and seal). We need the teachings and precepts that come from doctrinal instruction and discussion; we are saved no faster than we get knowledge, the Prophet Joseph told us.[6] And we need the leaders of the Church, both general and local—yes, for their supervision and direction, but also to obtain that divine power and strength that come through humbly acknowledging and following the counsel of those holding the keys.

It is inevitable in a lay church like ours (and that is exactly what the first-century Christian Church and the early restored Church were), that we will come face to face with differences in point of view, oddities and peculiarities, and even serious mistakes. It is hard to imagine that a member of the restored Church would not have several occasions during a lifetime when decisions were made with which he or she disagreed; when policies or procedures were put in place that rubbed him or her the wrong way; when the leadership style of a new bishop or stake president made him or her extremely uncomfortable. That comes with the turf of mortality, doesn't it?

We must remind ourselves frequently that God calls his prophets. Being called as a general authority, however, does not elevate one above mortality. President Dieter F. Uchtdorf declared: "Some struggle with unanswered questions about things that have been done or said in the past. We openly acknowledge that in nearly 200 years of Church history—along with an uninterrupted line of inspired, honorable, and divine events—there have been some things said and done that could cause people to question. . . .

"And, to be perfectly frank, there have been times when members or leaders in the Church have simply made mistakes. There may have been things said or done that were not in harmony with our values, principles, or doctrine.

"I suppose the Church would be perfect," President Uchtdorf observed, "only if it were run by perfect beings. God is perfect, and His doctrine is pure. But He works through us—His imperfect children—and imperfect people make mistakes."[7]

In the meridian of time, when Jesus had selected, prepared, and ordained his chosen apostles, he sent them out to carry the good news that the Promised Messiah, the Hope of Israel, had arrived, that the kingdom of God was now among them. These noble apostles were commissioned to bear solemn witness to the known world that peace and joy in this life and eternal reward in the life to come would depend on their willingness to receive this Messiah, receive the requisite covenants and ordinances, and put first in their lives the things pertaining to the kingdom of God. Jesus was their Principal, and the apostles were his agents. In our dispensation the Lord declared: "Wherefore, as ye are agents, ye are on the Lord's errand; and whatever ye do according to the will of the Lord is the Lord's business" (D&C 64:29).

Moreover, the Master uttered these unusual words: "He that receiveth you receiveth me, and he that receiveth me receiveth him that sent me" (Matthew 10:40). That is, the Principal sent his agents into the world to represent him, to speak his words and deliver his message; their word was to be interpreted as his word. Theirs was a divine investiture of authority, Jesus's authority, which, of course, was the authority of God the Father. Earlier the Lord had explained to these agents that "when they deliver you up, take no thought how or what ye shall speak: for it shall be given you in that same hour what ye shall speak. For *it is not ye that speak, but the Spirit of your Father which speaketh in you*" (Matthew 10:19–20; emphasis added; compare D&C 84:36–37). In our dispensation, a similar message, poignant in its implications, was delivered to Thomas B. Marsh, at the time he was serving as President of the Quorum of the Twelve Apostles: "Whosoever receiveth my word receiveth me, and *whoever receiveth me, receiveth those, the First Presidency, whom I have sent,* whom I have made counselors for my name's sake unto you" (D&C 112:20; emphasis added).

Decades ago, my mentor and friend Bob Matthews remarked to me that "the great tendency in the religious world and with religious scholars is to be just one dispensation behind!" That's a terribly astute observation. Thus to receive Peter, to listen to his message, and abide by his counsel was to listen to and obey the Lord Jesus, Peter's Principal. To give ear to what the apostle Paul had to say throughout Italy, Greece, and Asia Minor was to attend carefully to the words of the One who had struck down and turned around Saul of Tarsus on the road to Damascus. To spurn the message of Simon Peter or to ignore or even take lightly the oracles of his apostolic colleague Paul was to turn a deaf ear to the Lord and God of both Jew and Gentile, of both the living and the dead.

On more than one occasion when I was a missionary serving in the Eastern States Mission, we had the privilege of hearing from President Harold B. Lee, then a member of the Quorum of the Twelve Apostles. Elder Lee traveled to New York City frequently to attend meetings of boards on which he served, and he would often stop by the mission home, meet with our mission president, and spend time with the missionaries. One bit of his counsel was especially meaningful to me: "Elders and Sisters," he said, "I sense that not all of you have the kind of testimony that you would like to have. I sense that some of you are a bit hesitant to say with boldness, 'I know.' Well, let me say this: If you don't know for sure, then *you lean on my testimony, for I do know.*" I always felt something profound in his simple words: I knew he knew; he knew in ways I couldn't really comprehend at the time.

No man or woman is an island. We need never walk alone, for we are not alone. Further, we need not see dependence on others as a sign of weakness. It is not. In some ways, it is a sign of strength, and certainly an evidence of humility. It is significant that the Savior regards this willingness to lean upon the faith of others to be a spiritual gift: "To some it is given by the Holy Ghost to know that Jesus Christ is the Son of God, and that he was crucified for the sins of the world. *To others it is given to believe on their words, that they also might have eternal life if they continue faithful*" (D&C 46:13–14; emphasis added). To some extent, mortals will always lean on others, but, as we mentioned earlier, each one of us should be striving to acquire an independent witness of the truth.

I know in my mind and in my heart that we are engaged in the work of the Almighty and that his hand is over it. I have not always known with that certainty, however, for I leaned many times on the testimony of Uncle Joseph, Mom and Dad, and a host of witnesses who had come to know for themselves. Theirs was a strong, stabilizing influence in my life, an oasis of answers and assurance in what could have been a desert of doubt. In addition, it has been my privilege and opportunity to work closely with marvelous men and women in the Church Educational System who know the gospel is true, and they know the gospel.

Because of my work in Religious Education at Brigham Young University for more than thirty years, and particularly during the decade I served as dean, it was my sweet privilege to come to know several of the general Church leaders and to feel the power of their apostolic testimonies. It is clear beyond dispute that they know, they know they know, and that awareness provides a confidence and a humble boldness that empowers them to stand as witnesses of the name of Christ in all the world. Now these are some pretty impressive folks, men who are bright and energetic and quick, men who could be using their education and training to lead major corporations, be esteemed physicians, preside over colleges and universities, serve as state or federal judges, etc. And yet they have put aside worldly pursuits and aspirations in response to a call from a prophet, a call that they sensed and frequently testify came from God.

Are we to suppose they have all been duped? Hypnotized? Brainwashed? That they have been pressured in some way to assume a role that demands a completely consecrated life, to spend almost every weekend away from their home ward and their family? Hardly! Even though I have a witness of my own, even though my conviction lies deep within the inner recesses of my soul, I still lean on these great men—prophets, seers, and revelators. I look to them, I listen to them, I love them, I study their words carefully and regularly. God is my Father and Jesus is my

Lord and Savior, and my worship is reserved for them, but these apostolic Church leaders are like Matthew and Thomas and John and Bartholomew in the first century—they are the chosen and ordained servants of the Lord Jesus, and they deserve my respect, my allegiance, and my trust. When I am tempted to worry and fret over some troublesome matter, I often ask myself: Would President Hinckley or President Monson be troubled by this issue? Would Elder Oaks be stumped, befuddled, or anxious about that question? Would Elder Holland be knocked off center by that situation? Because the Spirit has borne witness to me that they are exactly what and who we sustain and uphold them to be, I take comfort in their assurance. I have a conviction of my own, but I rest easy because they refuse to take counsel from their fears. I am more at peace because they are at peace.

Conclusion

To have faith is to be loyal, live faithfully, to strive to become steadfast and immovable (1 Corinthians 15:58; Mosiah 5:15). It is to hold on, to hold fast, particularly in moments or seasons of spiritual unrest. "I had actually seen a vision," Joseph Smith declared; "and who am I that I can withstand God, or why does the world think to make me deny what I have actually seen? For I had seen a vision; I knew it, and I knew that God knew it, and I could not deny it, neither dared I do it; at least I knew that by so doing I would offend God, and come under condemnation" (Joseph Smith–History 1:25).

Faith is not just a belief, not just a sentiment. It is also an action, a behavior. Professor Adam Miller explained that "faith is more like being loyal to your husband or wife than it is like believing in magic." He also encouraged us: "When your faith falters and you're tempted to run, stand up and bear testimony instead. A testimony is a promise to stay. . . . *It is less a measure of your certainty about a list of facts than it is a mark of your commitment to bearing the truths that, despite their weakness, keep imposing themselves as a grace."*[8]

A man or woman who continues to demonstrate faith, particularly in the refiner's fire of intellectual and spiritual challenges to that faith, acquires an unusual strength, grows in subtle but significant ways. "As man's thoughts turn to God and the things that pertain to God," President Howard W. Hunter testified, "man undergoes a spiritual transformation." That faith "lifts him from the commonplace and gives to him a noble and Godlike character. . . . The most powerful force in human nature is the spiritual power of faith."[9]

We cleave to our faith because it is precious. We rejoice in the truth that God has chosen to bestow upon us this gift of the Spirit (1 Corinthians 12:9; Moroni 10:11; D&C 46:19–20). We are forever grateful that when we pass through turmoil and our faith seems to fade or falter, a gracious Lord is more than willing to walk patiently with us until our trust and confidence have been renewed.

Chapter 8

THE TRIAL
OF OUR FAITH

Few scenes in the Book of Mormon are more tragic than those of the Jaredites in the days of Coriantumr the king and Ether the prophet. The earth was filled with violence, and the order of the day was war and bloodshed. Ether "did cry from the morning, even until the going down of the sun, exhorting the people to believe in God unto repentance lest they should be destroyed, saying unto them that by faith all things are fulfilled. . . . And it came to pass that Ether did prophesy great and marvelous things unto the people, which they did not believe, because they saw them not" (Ether 12:3, 5). How typical. How familiar. As we have discussed, as people distance themselves from Deity, they gradually overlook, disregard, marginalize, and eventually dismiss completely the supernatural, the world that exists above and beyond the natural world. They believe only in that which they may perceive by means of the five senses.

Sadly, those five senses cannot discern those matters that are of infinite and eternal worth. The apostle Paul said it well when he wrote that "the natural man receiveth not the things of the Spirit of God: for they are foolishness unto him: neither can he know them, because they are spiritually discerned" (1 Corinthians 2:14). Moroni, the narrator in the book of Ether, then delivers one of the most profound principles in all of holy writ, one that has particular relevance to our study: "And now, I, Moroni, would speak somewhat concerning these things; I would show unto the world that faith is things which are hoped for and not seen; wherefore, dispute not because ye see not, for *ye receive no witness until after the trial of your faith*" (Ether 12:6; emphasis added).

Do, Then Know

The trial of our faith can obviously take many forms. For a person investigating the restored gospel, it may take the form of local ministers showing up with brochures and DVDs intended to attack, confuse, and create doubts during this time when these truth seekers are meeting regularly with the missionaries. For the new convert, it may take the form of having everything in the world go wrong during the weeks following the baptism—loss of employment, a car that breaks down and leaves them stranded, a spouse who becomes overly critical of the message of the Restoration, severe temptations to violate the word of wisdom, and a host of other problems.

A corollary of this principle was taught by Jesus when he announced: "My doctrine is not mine, but his that sent me. *If any man will do* [God's] will, *he shall know* of the doctrine, whether it be of God, or whether I speak of myself" (John 7:16–17). The concept is simple enough: DO and then KNOW. In other words, we come to know the truthfulness of a principle, a law, a commandment by abiding by it, by *testing* it, by *trying* it. Persons who confess that they really do not have much of a testimony of the law of the fast are generally encouraged to fast, with a purpose, coupled with regular prayer during the period of fasting. At the end of the fast, they ought to then reassess the matter. Persons who question the value of the law of tithing are encouraged to pay a full tithing, and, in the words of Jehovah through Malachi, prove the Lord, put him and his law of finance to the test. That is, be attentive, first and foremost, to revelation and divine insight or direction, be particularly sensitive to the receipt of what the Lord calls elsewhere, "wisdom and great treasures of knowledge, even hidden treasures" (D&C 89:19).

Alma provided some of the most beautiful instruction on acquiring and growing in faith of anything in scripture. Everyone who has read the Book of Mormon knows of his encouragement to plant the seed of faith. This seed is not just any seed; in its scriptural context, the seed is Christ, the understanding that Jesus "will come to redeem his people, and that he shall suffer and die to atone for their sins; and that he shall rise again from the dead, which shall bring to pass the resurrection, that all men shall stand before him, to be judged at the last and judgment day, according to their works. And now, my brethren," Alma comes to the point, "I desire that *ye shall plant this word in your hearts, and as it beginneth to swell even so nourish it by your faith. And behold, it will become a tree, springing up in you unto everlasting life. And then may God grant unto you that your burdens may be light* [compare Matthew 11:28–30], *through the joy of his Son*" (Alma 33:22–23; emphasis added).

Earlier in this discourse, Alma teaches a lesson that is priceless. Having planted the seed of faith—the knowledge that the Messiah will redeem humanity from sin and death—we begin to notice the early stages of the testimony of Jesus. It will swell within the breast, enlarge the soul, enlighten the understanding, and be "delicious" to the one performing the spiritual experiment. Alma then comments: "And now, behold, will not this strengthen your faith? Yea, it will strengthen your faith. . . . And now, behold, are ye sure that this is a good seed? I say unto you,

Yea." Now note this marvelous insight: "For *every seed bringeth forth unto its own likeness*" (Alma 32:28, 30–31; emphasis added).

Now, if as Alma has explained, the seed is specifically the word, the testimony of Jesus the Savior, how does that seed bring forth "unto its own likeness"? Reflecting regularly on the person of Jesus of Nazareth; contemplating the eternal significance of his singular mission; meditating on his infinite atoning sufferings and his ignominious death on the cruel cross of Calvary; expressing consistently the unending gratitude and love you feel because of the terrible price paid for your soul; and striving to emulate the life of the sinless Son of Man—by doing such things, the man or woman performing the experiment will begin to be *transformed into the likeness of Christ*. As Elder David A. Bednar testified, they will retain a remission of sins from day to day (Mosiah 4:11–12),[1] they will feel a deep need to love and serve those about them, will bear witness by both word and deed of the goodness of God, and will find themselves developing a Christian character. They will have tried the virtue and power of the Word. Further, when one has grown into faith he or she will, like Nephi, GO and DO (1 Nephi 3:7). In short, the path of the disciple of Christ is to do and then come to know, and then to know in more and more ways, and then continue to do. This is the cycle of faith.

The Fiery Trial

The Prophet Daniel's three noble associates—Shadrach, Meshach, and Abed-nego—were men of faith and righteous determination, just as was Daniel. They were also terribly loyal to Jehovah, the God of the patriarchs Abraham, Isaac, and Jacob, the God of Moses and the children of Israel. Having been carried into Babylonian captivity, they soon found themselves in difficult straits: they were repeatedly ordered to do that which had been forbidden by their God. They had refused to eat King

Nebuchadnezzar's rich food, but now they were really put to the test: they were commanded to worship and serve the gods of the Babylonians, which thing, of course, they would not do. They were informed that when they heard the sound of the cornet, flute, harp, and other musical instruments, they were to fall down and worship the image, the idol. If they refused, they would be cast into a "burning fiery furnace." Their inspiring reply to the king is classic: "If it be so, our God whom we serve is able to deliver us from the burning fiery furnace, and he will deliver us out of thine hand, O king." One could interrupt the narrative at that point and delight in the amazing faith of these ancient disciples. They were confident that God keeps his promises. Their faith was solid and sure.

The story does not, however, end there. For Shadrach, Meshach, and Abed-nego continued their speech: "*But if not*, be it known unto thee, O king, that we will not serve thy gods, nor worship the golden image which thou hast set up" (Daniel 3:14–18; emphasis added). They were only three words—but if not—but they spoke volumes about the depth of these young men's faith, the depth of their testimony of their Lord and God, the depth of their everlasting covenant to worship no other Gods. To reflect on their words, they were saying, in essence, "We will not worship a false God, and we are persuaded that our God, the true and living God, has the power to deliver us from the flames, and will do so if it is in keeping with his omniscient mind and contributes in some way to the furtherance of his eternal purposes." Then a pause, a few seconds of sober reflection, followed by, "But if our God should choose not to deliver us, to keep us from perishing in the flames, then we glory in his wise decision. And, knowing that we may be facing our death, we affirm that we worship Jehovah and him alone; we will not worship your golden image." Reflect for a moment on those simple but momentous words, *But if not*. "There will be times in each of our lives," Elder Neal A. Maxwell taught, "when our faith must not be conditioned upon God's rescuing or relieving us, because in fact He may not—at least, not as we would choose to be rescued."[2]

The brethren who attended the School of the Elders in the winter of 1834–35 were taught: "For a man to lay down his all, his character and reputation, his honor, and applause, his good name among men, his houses, his lands, his brothers and sisters, his wife and children, and even his own life also—counting all things but filth and dross for the excellency of the knowledge of Jesus Christ—requires more than mere belief or supposition that he is doing the will of God; but actual knowledge, realizing that, when these sufferings are ended, he will enter into eternal rest, and be a partaker of the glory of God."[3] The three righteous men we have been discussing didn't just "think" they were doing the right thing. They didn't merely "hope" they could avoid the flames. Rather, they had resolved in their hearts to "be guided and directed by his will," so that "nothing short of an actual knowledge of . . . their having embraced the order of things which God has established for the redemption of man" would give to them "that confidence in him, necessary for them to overcome the world, and obtain that crown of glory which is laid up for them that fear God."[4]

In these same lectures is contained an utterance that is perhaps the most-often quoted and most beloved in Mormonism: "Let us here observe, that *a religion that does not require the sacrifice of all things never has power sufficient to produce the faith necessary unto life and salvation*."[5] Why is this the case? Because only a church that will ask everything of its members—everything!—is in a position to promise its members the riches of eternity. Unconditional surrender is always prerequisite to total victory. Only those who reach the point in their spiritual development

where they are at last willing and able to fully consecrate themselves to the Lord and his Church and kingdom, and to do so
without hesitation, can gain that confidence before God that results in the promise of eternal life. In speaking of the ancients,
the elders were instructed that "through the knowledge thus obtained [that their course in life was in harmony with the divine
will] their faith became sufficiently strong to lay hold upon the
promise of eternal life, . . . and obtain the end of their faith, even
the salvation of their souls."[6]

There are times when faith requires us to act in the face of
(what the world would consider to be) the absurd. Abraham was
asked to put to death his beloved and long-awaited son Isaac,
the one hope Abraham had of fulfilling the promise that his posterity would be as numerous as the sands upon the seashore or
the stars in the heavens. Jehovah had spoken. Abraham was well
acquainted with the voice of the Lord and knew that what had
been commanded did in fact come from God. There was, however, something more he needed to know.

Professor Truman Madsen spoke of being a guide in the
Holy Land for President Hugh B. Brown, an apostle who also
served for a number of years as a counselor to President David O.
McKay. While walking in Hebron, where the traditional tomb
of Abraham is found, Professor Madsen asked, "'What are the
blessings of Abraham, Isaac, and Jacob?' Elder Brown thought a
moment and answered in one word, 'Posterity.' Then I almost
burst out, 'Why, then, was Abraham commanded to go to Mount
Moriah and offer his only hope of posterity?'

"It was clear that this man, nearly ninety, had thought and
prayed and wept over that question before. He finally said,
'Abraham needed to learn something about Abraham.'"[7] When the
awful assignment came to offer up Isaac in sacrifice, he obeyed,
even though, rationally speaking, there was no way the divine

promises could thereafter be realized. But the man known as the Father of the Faithful had implicit trust in his Lord, "accounting that God was able to raise [Isaac] up, even from the dead" (Hebrews 11:19). Abraham knew God and he knew His purposes; the finite mind yielded to the Infinite. His "leap of faith" was prerequisite to his ascent to glory. What he then knew about himself was that there was nothing the Almighty could request of him with which he would not obediently comply. Because he was willing to sacrifice that which was precious and priceless to himself, he grew into a faith that was solid, secure, and unshakable.[8]

Elder David A. Bednar spoke admiringly of Elder Maxwell as follows: "In October 1997, Sister Bednar and I hosted Elder and Sister Maxwell at Brigham Young University–Idaho. Elder Maxwell was to speak to the students, staff, and faculty in a devotional assembly.

"Earlier in that same year, Elder Maxwell underwent 46 days and nights of debilitating chemotherapy for leukemia. His rehabilitation and continued therapy progressed positively through the spring and summer months, but Elder Maxwell's physical strength and stamina were nonetheless limited when he traveled to Rexburg. After greeting Elder and Sister Maxwell at the airport, Susan and I drove them to our home for rest and a light lunch before the devotional.

"I asked Elder Maxwell what lessons he had learned through his illness. I will remember always the precise and penetrating answer he gave. 'Dave,' he said, 'I have learned that *not shrinking is more important than surviving.*'"[9] Or, as Elder Maxwell had put it on a previous occasion, "The submission of one's will is placing on God's altar the only uniquely personal thing one has to place there."[10]

A Personal Struggle

During the late 1980s I had the opportunity to serve as the first counselor in a Brigham Young University campus stake presidency. It was a wonderful period of years to work with men in the presidency whom I admired greatly; to meet regularly with the high council and benefit from their extensive experience in life and in the Church; and to spend many hours serving joyously with a remarkable group of dedicated bishops. There's just no question about it—I learned far more than I taught. Our stake president was a beloved and longtime friend; we had worked together in Seminaries and Institutes, and the two of us were hired the same year as members of the faculty in BYU Religious Education. I was also the associate department chair to this great and good man. He blessed my life in many important ways.

We had been serving as a presidency for only two years when our president was invited to be the director of the BYU Jerusalem Center. This meant, of course, that he and his wife would need to move to Jerusalem and, as pertaining to our stake assignment, that he would be released and the stake presidency reorganized. It was sad to learn this from the president, although I was "Church broke" enough to know that releases come just as do calls, and that members are expected to be flexible and spiritually resilient when it comes to working in the kingdom.

We moved ahead as a presidency as though nothing would change, although we realized that in two months the presidency would be dissolved. The three of us wanted to finish strong. About a month before the date of the stake conference where the changes would be made, I began having feelings and even what I perceived to be spiritual nudges that I would be called as the stake president. I fought them—not because I wouldn't accept the call if it came, but because I definitely did not want to aspire to anything, especially something as serious and involved as this position would be. The feelings grew stronger as we moved toward the date. I found myself many a night awake at 3:00 am and walking out to our back porch. There I would pour out my heart to the Lord as earnestly and intently as I could. My words seemed to be the same with every trip to the porch: "Please know that I do not want this if it is not something to which I should not and will not be called. And yet I will do whatever I am called to do. I just don't want to be inappropriate or to be self-deceived in any way." Only a couple of days before the stake conference I had a dream. I dreamt that I had been called as the stake president and that I was being set apart by Elder Vaughn J. Featherstone of the Seventy. (At this point, we were not exactly sure which member of the Seventy would accompany Elder David B. Haight of the Quorum of the Twelve Apostles.) When I awoke from the dream, I made my way back to the back porch (I was drawn to the porch because there I could speak aloud without waking anyone). I uttered the same concerns and yet offered to be obedient to whatever took place.

On the Saturday before the Sunday session, I received a phone call requesting that my wife Shauna and I meet with Elder Haight at the administration building on BYU campus. Our meeting with him was warm and pleasant. We returned home and were there for only a couple of hours when the phone rang again: it was Elder Haight. He said, "President Millet, I have felt impressed to call the second counselor to serve as the new president, and he has asked for you to serve as his first counselor. Would you be willing to assume that responsibility?" I responded that I would be happy to continue to serve with this wonderful man.

I was devastated, but not at all for what you may think—I was not troubled one bit about the fact that I wasn't called as stake president, *except*, that I could have been so mistaken, so deceived. I found myself doing some very serious introspection, asking for forgiveness for aspiring, for assuming what was not to be. The next day the main session of stake conference was probably wonderful, but I am ashamed to admit that I was so out of it spiritually and emotionally that I couldn't have enjoyed it. I went through the motions of participating in the meeting, including delivering one of the addresses. After the session and after an extended period when Elders Haight and Featherstone seemed to greet and shake hands with everyone (there were about 1500 in attendance), we moved upstairs in the Ernest L. Wilkinson Student Center for the settings apart. The new stake president was first set apart. Elder Haight pronounced a marvelous blessing upon his head, one that touched my heart deeply; I felt so very pleased for my dear friend, and for a few moments the gloom surrounding my soul seemed to lift. Next Elder Haight motioned for me to come forward and be seated in front of the Church leaders.

Once I sat down, the Brethren (and the new stake president, who was invited to join in the circle) laid their hands on my head. There was a pause, and then Elder Haight leaned down close to me and whispered in my ear: "Brother Millet, the Lord certainly loves you." Then hands were re-placed, but again there was a short pause, followed by Elder Haight saying, "No, I think Elder Featherstone should set you apart." As he did so, scenes from the dream I had had only a couple of days before flooded my mind. I wept through the entire experience, following which both of the general authorities embraced me. The new stake presidency received some valuable counsel from the Church leaders, after which we agreed as a presidency to meet the following Wednesday for our regular presidency meeting, and then separated. To some extent, my feelings of deep disappointment abated for the remainder of the day, and I did indeed feel the love of my Heavenly Father throughout the day and into the evening.

As time went by, I functioned as always in my Church calling and did all in my power to support our new stake president. But deep within my soul I was not at peace. Any feelings of self-confidence were gone, as well as any feelings of spiritual assurance. In moments here and there throughout the next few weeks I found myself asking: "How could you have been so very wrong? How could you have missed this so badly? What else have you missed? What divine answers and 'spiritual certainties' that you have received over the years may well have been self-fulfilling?" O how I questioned myself, my capacity to feel or know the Spirit of the Lord, to discern the mind and will of the Lord.

At the end of the first month things seemed to be coming to a head. I had continued to pray, to fast, to plead for God's help, to yearn for a feeling that he was still there and that he had not forsaken me. My faith was being stretched in ways that I had never known, in a manner that was emotionally draining and spiritually stifling. Late one night as I knelt, broken and exhausted in my despair, I felt an infusion of something, almost anger, toward God and this whole situation. I poured out my heart and laid out in detail all the things that had been weighing on me. As I recall, the words I spoke were something like the following: "Father, I know that you live and that this work in which we are engaged is in fact your work. I don't doubt this at all. But I do doubt myself, terribly. And I don't want to feel this way any longer. My stake president deserves better than this. My wife and children need a husband and a father that is strong, firm, and solid in the faith. And I want to be that kind of person again." At this point I felt almost a spirit of quiet defiance come over me. I acknowledged to the Lord that I felt I had been passing through a test of some kind that is not like anything I had ever known. I stated that I had sincerely tried to be the right kind of man, but today the heavens felt like brass over my head. Through my tears I cried out (and these words I remember perfectly): "But though you slay me, yet will I trust in you."

The first thing I felt was surprise at my irreverence and audacity, and then embarrassment for even the slightest suggestion that my paltry challenges were even in the same ballpark with those faced by Job (see Job 13:15). The next feeling that came to me, however, was one of a settling peace, as though a warm blanket had been wrapped around me. I had often wondered what the promise of Malachi was like, that God would "open you the windows of heaven, and pour you out a blessing, that there shall not be room enough to receive it" (Malachi 3:10). On this rare occasion, however, I felt the windows of heaven opened widely, and more than anything I sensed clearly and keenly the pure love of the Lord Jesus Christ. Normally I would add here that I did not hear a voice, but my subsequent gospel study compels me to say otherwise. Note the Lord's language in the revelation we call the Olive Leaf: "Behold, that which you hear is as the voice of one crying in the wilderness—in the wilderness, because you cannot see him—*my voice, because my voice is Spirit*; my Spirit is truth" (D&C 88:66; emphasis added). In that sweet sense, I did indeed hear the voice of God.

Even after decades of time have passed, I still do not know all the reasons why I was mistaken regarding the calling to serve as a stake president. Interestingly, I have since served in that capacity. No, this experience is not exactly the same as that trial through which a member of the Church passes when he or she has begun to doubt the prophetic call of Joseph Smith or in general the truthfulness of the restored gospel. But the nature of the anguish, the extensive suffering through periods of seeming alienation, the darkness of mind and pain of personally doubting one's own spiritual perceptions is no less traumatic. I do not know completely what purpose this whole episode served in my life, except that I know, to some extent at least, that I passed through a trial of my faith, one that has yielded some valuable fruit. If for no other reason, I feel compassion and can identify more closely with someone who feels forsaken, or lost, or deeply troubled about their faith.

I do know that the God who has spoken *still speaks, will speak again and again*. We just need to have patience, faith, and the ears to listen. We may well need to invite and then allow our heart to tell our mind some things it did not know, and it may take some time for our minds—our rational faculties—to catch up with our feelings. The result will, however, almost always be worth the wait.

Conclusion

As Christians, our aspiration is to emulate, to imitate the life of the only truly sinless person to walk this earth. Now if Christ's pathway to Godhood was so unimaginably painful and difficult, why would we suppose that we should be insulated against hard things and hard times? The scriptures teach that his disciples are called upon to suffer with him, indeed to enter the "fellowship of his sufferings" (Philippians 3:10). One of the keys to eventually becoming "heirs of God, and joint-heirs with Christ" is being willing to "suffer with him" (Romans 8:17).

Why then would we bristle at the thought of being tried and tested here on earth? Why would we, even in the apogee of our agony, rail and pout at God? To be sure, few of us are excited to engage our next trial, just around the corner. An acquaintance once mentioned to me that because of the learning and growth and development that can come through overcoming trials, he prays for them. Well, personally, you wouldn't catch me dead praying for trials! They come on their own. They are much like weeds in a garden: they pop up just fine without our planting them. "Sufficient unto the day is the evil thereof," the Lord said (Matthew 6:34).

Isn't facing and enduring and overcoming trials largely why we took a physical body in the first place? Returning to Peter, we read: "Beloved, think it not strange concerning the fiery trial which is to try you, as though some strange thing happened unto you: But rejoice, inasmuch as ye are partakers of Christ's sufferings; that, when his glory shall be revealed, ye may be glad also with exceeding joy" (1 Peter 4:12–13). Trials come with the turf of the second estate.

President Thomas S. Monson taught, "It was not raining when Noah was commanded to build an ark. Two Heavenly Personages were not yet seen when Joseph knelt and prayed. There was no visible ram in the thicket when Abraham prepared to sacrifice his son Isaac. First came the test of faith, and then the miracle.

"Remember that faith and doubt cannot exist in the same mind at the same time, for one will dispel the other. Cast out doubt. Cultivate faith. Strive always to retain that childlike faith which can move mountains and bring heaven closer to heart and home."[11]

As everyone knows very well, those trials come in all shapes and sizes and colors, and they come throughout our life. One of them is, of course, the trials that come to our faith, that lean on us from time to time, that buffet us throughout life, that beckon us to yield to fear and doubt, to panic and run. To some extent, these may prove to be the most painful and debilitating of all. As I have attempted to point out, it is not necessary for one to doubt, nor is doubt a prerequisite for faith. The Lord our God is merciful, and he is infinitely understanding, including understanding our spiritual pain, our confusion, and our emptiness. As it is with our temporal torments, so it is with our spiritual suffering: he will "comfort [our] souls in Christ" (Alma 31:32), will send peace and calm to replace our anxiety, and in process of time will lead us to find either answers or at least temporary resolutions to our concerns. Of that I am a personal witness.

Chapter 9

"ALL THINGS SHALL WORK TOGETHER"

In his first epistle to the Corinthian Saints, the apostle Paul speaks at some length about the gifts of the Spirit, including which of those gifts are of greatest value in edifying the members of the Church of Jesus Christ. The twelfth chapter ends with this verse: "But covet earnestly [be zealous for] the best gifts: and yet shew I unto you a more excellent way" (1 Corinthians 12:31). What follows, of course, is a beautifully crafted and beloved sermonette on charity, which Mormon calls "the pure love of Christ" (Moroni 7:47). Toward the end of what is to us the thirteenth chapter, Paul writes: "When I was a child, I spake as a child, I understood as a child, I thought as a child: but when I became a man, I put away childish things" (v. 11). This verse has been employed by Christians through the centuries to teach a variety of lessons, not the least of which is the need for people to grow up, to set aside matters of lesser worth. In its context, however, Paul appears to be instructing the Corinthians that greater than tongues, healing, discerning of spirits, grander than wisdom, knowledge, and even prophecy, is charity, which is God-like love, the very love that Jesus Christ has demonstrated so abundantly and perfectly toward all of us (Ether 12:33–34). I believe Paul was calling the former-day Saints to Christian maturity, the kind of maturity in which God-fearing people have become spontaneously tender and loving toward the children of God.

Things Will Work Out

A most fascinating verse in 1 Corinthians 13 is verse 12: "For now we see through a glass, darkly; but then face to face: now I know in part; but then shall I know even as also I am known." Latter-day Saints use this verse to refer to the veil of forgetfulness that is placed upon our minds as we leave the first estate and enter the second estate by birth. You might find other translations of this passage worthwhile:

"We see in a mirror, dimly" (New Revised Standard Version);

"Now we see but a poor reflection" (New International Version);

"At the moment all that we can see are puzzling reflections in a mirror" (Wright, *Kingdom New Testament*);

"We don't yet see things clearly. We're squinting in a fog, peering through a mist" (Peterson, *The Message*).

It's as though Paul is reminding the disciples that in this life we don't have the whole picture; we are, for now, kept from seeing and understanding the end from the beginning. For the time being, that grand panoramic scene is reserved for God and a few of his anointed servants, often dispensation heads like Enoch (Moses 6–7), Abraham (Abraham 3), Moses (Moses 1), and Joseph Smith (D&C 76).

One of the painful results of having an incomplete picture is that we cannot see at once how a given moment or series of events in our lives fit into the larger scheme of things. This is particularly true when we face mortal challenges and tragedies. The seeming enormity and, in some cases, finality of a given vicissitude in this life can overwhelm us when we are fixated on the present and lose that elevated perspective that comes only from God. When, for example, a mother and her six children learn that their father has been taken in death, it is extremely difficult, almost impossible, to see anything but the painful present and feel nothing but despair and even hopelessness toward the future. What that mother and her children cannot see is how they will get by, how they will have the money to sustain their needs, how Mom and the remaining family will survive. In those traumatic, emotionally strangling seasons, few of us would be able to fathom how things will ever work out.

That same meridian apostle wrote to the Romans: "And we know that all things work together for good to them that love God, to them who are called according to his purpose" (Romans 8:28). It's mighty tough to grasp how a tragedy of the magnitude of the one mentioned above will ever "work together for good" in their lives. To be sure, God does not send all of the trials that come into our lives. Some of them we bring upon ourselves through mismanagement of our lives, and others come to us as a result of other persons' unwise or even evil misuse of their moral agency. Paul's message here, a message sounded beautifully in Restoration scripture, is that God can cause things to work together for our good. Being omniscient, omnipotent, and, by the power of his Holy Spirit, omnipresent, our Father in heaven can, if we will let him, turn the most miserable of life's losses toward our eventual gain.

This is what Lehi meant when he consoled his son Jacob: "Jacob, my firstborn in the wilderness, thou knowest the greatness of God; and he shall consecrate thine afflictions for thy gain" (2 Nephi 2:2). That same Jacob, in engraving some of his own doings and teachings, observed: "Look unto God with firmness of mind, and pray unto him with exceeding faith, and he will console you in your afflictions" (Jacob 3:1). As Amulon began to intensify his abuse and persecution on Alma's people, the voice of the Lord came to the people: "I will . . . ease the burdens which are put upon your shoulders, that even you cannot feel them upon your backs, even while you are in bondage [or pain or distress or depression]; and this will I do that ye may stand as witnesses for me hereafter, and that ye may know of a surety that I, the Lord God, do visit my people in their afflictions" (Mosiah 24:14). It was in Liberty Jail that the Prophet Joseph Smith penned a letter to the Saints in which he pleaded to God for divine intervention. The Lord's response was: "My son, peace be unto thy soul; thine adversity and thine afflictions shall be but a small moment" (D&C 121:7). Truman Madsen reminded us that "That 'small moment' turned out to be five more years of incredible struggle. But comparatively, it was a small moment. And that, I submit to you, is a real force in facing suffering. To believe, better, to know that this lonely or crushed or deprived or painwracked condition won't last forever; that it will somehow, somewhere be over, is a balm of comfort. Without it, certain kinds of suffering would be unbearable."[1]

Later, after recording every conceivable horrendous situation into which Joseph might be thrust, the Savior inspired the Prophet to add that, "above all, if the very jaws of hell shall gape open the mouth wide after thee, know thou, my son, that all these things shall give thee experience, and shall be for thy good" (D&C 122:7). "Life is an obstacle course," Truman Madsen pointed out. "And sometimes it is a spook alley. But the before was a time for visioning the after. And some of our prayers are like the gambler's, 'Give me the money I made you promise not to give me if I asked for it.' What does a true friend do in such a case? God will honor our first request, to let us go through it; and He will provide you with (let Him) the way to make it bearable. More, to make it productive."[2]

At the funeral of President Gordon B. Hinckley, President Henry B. Eyring stated: "I heard [President Hinckley's] voice so many times when a difficult problem facing the Church was brought to him. He would listen carefully, perhaps asking a question or two, to be sure he understood the magnitude of the difficulty facing us and that those who brought the problem to him knew he understood. Time after time, he would quietly say something like this, with a pleasant smile, 'Oh, things will work out.'

"He was an optimist. Some of that came from his great personal capacities. Many problems he could work out himself. . . . *That unfailing confidence in the power of God shaped what he was able to see in the progress of the Lord's Church.* No one was more aware of problems than he. And yet time and again he would say of the Church that we have never done better, and he would give you facts to prove it. Then he would say with conviction in his voice, 'And the best is yet to come.'"[3]

Sister Neill F. Marriott, a member of the Young Women General Presidency, explained that many years ago "my husband, children, and I chose this family motto: 'It will all work out.' Yet how can we say those words to one another when deep troubles come and answers aren't readily available?" Sister Marriott then drew upon a personally difficult situation, the unexpected death of her 21-year-old daughter, Georgia. "Following Georgia's mortal death," she said, "our feelings were raw, we struggled, and still today we have moments of great sorrow, but we hold to the understanding that no one ever really dies. Despite our anguish when Georgia's physical body stopped functioning, we had faith that she went right on living as a spirit, and we believe we will live with her eternally if we adhere to our temple covenants." Sister Marriott then added: "Our family motto doesn't say, 'It will all work out *now*.' It speaks of our hope in the eternal outcome—not necessarily of present results."[4]

Search Diligently

In a revelation given to Joseph Smith in March 1833, the Savior challenged us to "search diligently, pray always, and be believing, and all things shall work together for your good, if ye walk uprightly and remember the covenant wherewith ye have covenanted one with another" (D&C 90:24). I believe this remarkable bit of counsel is crucial to how we should pursue answers to hard questions, how to handle difficult doctrinal matters, and how to gain perspective on historical events.

We are counseled first to *search diligently*. We search for answers. We dig. We research with energy. To be *diligent* in our search is to be "constant in effort," to "pursue with persevering attention," to be "painstaking," to be "tireless."[5] Clearly, to search diligently is not to be casual, laissez-faire, or haphazard. It is not to take a moment to glance here and peruse there, but instead is to undertake a steady, perhaps even systematic study. It is to read widely, as well as deeply. It is to become more conversant with what leaders of the Church or LDS scholars have written or spoken on touchy matters.

A few years ago while working at my desk in my BYU office, I received a phone call from a man in Salt Lake City. He introduced himself, spoke of the fact that he had been raised in the Church, had served a mission, been a bishop, and had presided, with his wife, over one of the missions of the Church. He explained that recently he had come across some writings about the history of the Church and then decided (before he had read them himself) that he would purchase copies for his family. The family had dived into the work and had not traveled very far into it when he and his children had begun to encounter what he described as "shocking" historical matters. He asked me, "Brother Millet, did you know that Joseph Smith practiced polygamy?" I replied: "Yes, I did know that." He came right back: "How long have you known that?" I was then rather startled, paused for a few seconds, and said, "Oh, I don't know exactly, but probably about fifty years." "Well I didn't know about it," he said, "and it was a real shocker for me and my children. Some of the family have begun to question their testimony of the restored gospel. Tell me, Brother Millet, why hadn't I encountered it before now?"

We spoke for a few minutes, I recommended some reading material for the family, and the conversation ended. I sat there stunned. I asked myself: How in this world could a person grow up in the heart of the Church, serve in responsible Church callings, and not know that Joseph Smith had indeed entered into plural marriage? How could a member of the Church read the Doctrine and Covenants and not know that? The correct and most direct answer to the brother's question was really, "I don't know why you have never heard of it before. In fact, I have trouble believing that you could travel this far in the Church and *not* know about it."

There are so many things with which active, faithful, curious, reading members of The Church of Jesus Christ of Latter-day Saints should be well acquainted. Members ought to be aware of and well acquainted with the "Gospel Topics" essays on lds.org, in which faithful LDS scholars were asked to address some of the more controversial and sensitive issues facing the Church. These essays were vetted and scrupulously reviewed at the highest levels of Church administration. They contain a wealth of information, and perhaps more important than the facts, they provide a perspective, a context for understanding the topic. "Yet however grateful we are for the information provided in these essays," Latter-day Saint scholar Patrick Mason pointed out, "we can't expect the church to do all the work for us. Just as we are accountable to "work out [our] own salvation" (Philippians 2:12), we have to take personal responsibility for how we will approach, process, and ultimately handle challenging issues in church history and doctrine."[6]

Mason stated that "we don't belong to a church of experts."[7] He is of course correct. So what do members of the Church do, after they have read and studied the Gospel Topics essays, prayed for divine guidance, and still come away not quite satisfied, not yet prepared to let the matter go? Elder M. Russell Ballard encouraged religious educators to teach their students "about the challenges they face when relying upon the Internet to answer questions of eternal significance. Remind them that James did not say, 'If any of you lack wisdom, let him [ask of] Google!'

"Wise people do not rely on the Internet to diagnose and treat emotional, mental, and physical health challenges, especially life-threatening challenges. Instead, they seek out health experts, those trained and licensed by recognized medical and state boards. Even then, prudent people seek a second opinion.

"If that is the sensible course to take in finding answers for emotional, mental, and physical health issues, it is even more so when eternal life is at stake. When something has the potential to threaten our spiritual life, our most precious family relationships, and our membership in the kingdom, we should find thoughtful and faithful Church leaders to help us. And, if necessary, we should ask those with appropriate academic training, experience, and expertise for help.

"This is exactly what I do when I need an answer to my own questions that I cannot answer myself. I seek help from my Brethren in the Quorum of the Twelve and from others with expertise in fields of Church history and doctrine."[8]

One other guiding principle is to consult the right kind of people. If one were eager to know more about Jesus, he or she might not be well served by confining their study to what Annas, Caiaphas, or Pontius Pilate had to say about the Savior.

Peter, James, and John, along with folks like Nicodemus, Mary Magdalene, and the sisters Mary and Martha would be especially helpful in acquiring accurate inside information. If my topic was the apostle Paul, then to spend the bulk of the interview time with the Judaizers or with Nero Caesar would be foolhardy.

If I felt driven to gain a deeper and more personal look into Joseph Smith the man, how lopsided and skewed would be my investigation if the bulk of my information came from Alexander Campbell, E. D. Howe, John C. Bennett, or William Law. Yes, it is often helpful to know what the critics and opponents have to say, but wouldn't those who knew the person intimately well be in a better position to comment and explain things? Similarly, if someone were genuinely seeking to find solutions to their doctrinal concerns or better explanations for sensitive historical moments, why would they want to immerse themselves in the writings or conversations of counter-cult groups, Ex-Mormons for Jesus, or persons who have left Mormonism but now cannot seem to leave it alone?

Pray Always

Sadly, when a person has fallen into serious sin or allowed himself or herself to be drowned in anti-Mormon propaganda or critiques by nonbelievers, too often the first thing that begins to slide is personal prayer. Odd, isn't it? God the Eternal Father is the ultimate object of our worship (D&C 20:17–19), the God and Father of Jesus Christ and of each one of us (John 20:17), the one true Source, the one Avenue where we go to learn for certain if something is of the Lord or of Lucifer. He is the Father of lights (James 1:17), the One eager to grant wisdom to all who seek it faithfully (James 1:5–6). Further, as Elder Neal A. Maxwell observed, "Unlike us, God has no restrictive office hours."[9] Surely there could not be a more compelling reason or a more propitious time for an individual who is searching or struggling with faith issues to intensify their prayers and spend appreciable time "listening" during and following prayer.

President Thomas S. Monson spoke of a personnel officer "assigned to handle petty grievances [who] concluded an unusually hectic day by placing facetiously a little sign on his desk for those with unsolved problems to read. It read, 'Have you tried prayer?'

"What that personnel director did not know when he placed such a sign upon his desk was that he was providing counsel and direction which would *solve more problems, alleviate more suffering, prevent more transgression, and bring about greater peace and contentment* in the human soul than could be obtained in any other way."[10]

When we are earnestly seeking to find answers from on high to our questions on historical or doctrinal matters, we are requesting information, insight, perspective, context, enlightenment. When we are seeking to alleviate the discomfort in our hearts and reduce the confusion in our minds, we pray to know where to look; we pray to see the greater and grander picture, to be given, as it is appropriate, a God's-eye view; we seek the Lord diligently to sense those to whom we should look for advice or direction. We pray for clarity, for composure, for comfort, for a calm spirit and a peaceful and satisfied mind. And this sacred endeavor isn't just about feelings, although our feelings are vital in coming to know the truth and gaining a witness of the truthfulness of the restored gospel. The Restoration is rigorous enough to withstand careful scrutiny, and each of us has a right to receive a witness, an understanding that is as satisfying to the mind as it is soothing and settling to the heart. "Brethren and sisters, I know that you are a praying people," President Hinckley declared. "That is a wonderful thing in this day and time when the practice of prayer has slipped from many lives. To call upon the Lord for wisdom beyond our own, for strength to do what we ought to do, for comfort and consolation, and for the expression of gratitude is a significant and wonderful thing."[11] On another occasion, President Hinckley said simply, "Believe in prayer and the power of prayer. Pray to the Lord with the expectation of answers." Finally, "Be prayerful. You cannot make it alone. You cannot reach your potential alone."[12]

Be Believing

A believing heart is a precious possession, a most worthwhile divine gift, especially in a day like our own. One who hears the servants of the Lord speak in general conference, for example, and who senses that what they are saying represents the mind and will of the Almighty is in a blessed condition, especially in a day of compounding unbelief. "Blessed are they who humble themselves without being compelled to be humble," Alma explained; "or rather, in other words, blessed is he that believeth in the word of God . . . without being brought to know the word, or even compelled to know, before they will believe" (Alma 32:16). Or as the Risen Lord said to Thomas, "because thou hast seen me, thou hast believed: blessed are they that have not seen"—which, of course, would be the overwhelming majority of members of the Church of Jesus Christ—"and yet have believed" (John 20:29).

It was Nephi, son of Lehi, who, "having great desires to know of the mysteries of God"—those sacred verities that can only be known by the power of the Holy Spirit—"did cry unto the Lord; and behold *he did visit me, and did soften my heart that I did believe all the words which had been spoken by my father*" (1 Nephi 2:16; emphasis added). No doubt many of us read these words carefully and are a bit surprised, for we know Nephi as a man who already had a heart that was receptive and attentive to spiritual realities. But we are all growing, day by day. Now notice what follows in the Book of Mormon: "*And I spake unto Sam, making known unto him the things which the Lord had manifested unto me* by his Holy

Spirit. And it came to pass that *he believed in my words*" (1 Nephi 2:17; emphasis added). Sam leaned on Nephi, sensed and felt assured by the Spirit that what his younger brother taught was true and from the Lord, and that crucial decision by Sam to believe impacted the remainder of the Nephite history.

Just before the conversion of Alma the younger and the sons of Mosiah, Mormon wrote that "there were many of the rising generation that could not understand the words of king Benjamin, being little children at the time he spake unto his people; and they did not believe the tradition of their fathers. They did not believe what had been said concerning the resurrection of the dead, neither did they believe concerning the coming of Christ." Some two decades had passed, and the "rising generation"—the young people, the youth—chose not to believe what their parents had felt and understood from King Benjamin's mighty sermon (Mosiah 2–4). Then followed this poignant insight from Mormon: "And now *because of their unbelief they could not understand the word of God;* and their hearts were hardened" (Mosiah 26:1–3; emphasis added).

Men and women who don't believe don't understand. People who have allowed their hearts to become hardened, who revel and even delight in cynicism, such people will forevermore fall short of what they might know and grasp, unless they repent. People who allow their questions to morph into doubts, and who delight in, and maybe even celebrate and parade those doubts, will never understand doctrines and principles that are beautifully plain to "the weak and the simple" (D&C 1:19, 23; 35:13). Those who have unanswered questions, who allow themselves to simmer in skepticism, and who eventually become hardened in their ignorance, are generally those who either chose to keep their questions to themselves, refused to admit their need for knowledge, and faced their fears alone, or instead turned in the wrong direction for help. In short, there are some people who, because of their refusal to believe, will never comprehend the truths of greatest worth. On the other hand, a boy or girl, a woman or man who has a believing heart—note, we are not speaking here of a gullible heart—will see and feel and grasp sacred matters that others whose minds are closed and whose hearts are hardened will never know. How glorious is the promise of the Lord: "And *whosoever shall believe* in my name, *doubting nothing, unto him* [or her] *will I confirm all my words*, even unto the ends of the earth" (Mormon 9:25; emphasis added).

Conclusion

Trials come. Challenges confront us regularly. And questions, tough questions arise in the lives of those who read and study and do serious thinking. Repeating the scripture with which we began this conversation: "Search diligently, pray always, and be believing, and all things shall work together for your good" (D&C 90:24). "This doesn't mean all things *are* good," Sister Marriott clarified, "but for the meek and faithful, things—both positive and negative—work together for good, and the timing is the Lord's. We wait on Him, sometimes like Job in his suffering. . . . A meek heart accepts the trial and the waiting for that time of healing and wholeness to come."[13]

It isn't that *we* can cause all things to work together for our good, although we certainly need to be open to the Lord's purposes unfolding in our individual universes. Rather, it is our Heavenly Father, Who, knowing all things and having all power, can coordinate the comings and goings of his children, can so orchestrate events and people and circumstances as to achieve the greatest possible good and the deepest happiness. Knowing that God is in charge is both liberating and calming!

Chapter 10

"WHAT GREATER WITNESS...?"

After Shauna and I had been dating off and on for about a year and a half, we sensed that the relationship was moving toward marriage. We discussed it and felt that it would be wise for us to devote a day to fasting and prayer to see how the Lord felt about things. We did so, and on the next day we met in the old Joseph Smith Building on the Brigham Young University campus. We used the four or five minutes before our large Book of Mormon class was to start to talk about how the fast had gone. I asked Shauna, "Well, how do you feel?"

She said simply, "Fine."

I responded, "No, I mean, how do you feel about getting married?"

She looked me in the eye and replied, "I said that I feel fine about it. How do you feel?"

I indicated that I felt good about it, as well.

I cannot speak for Shauna, but I admit that I felt either disappointed or underwhelmed—not in Shauna or about whether we should get married but in how our answer had come. I don't know that I expected bells and whistles or the appearance of a member of the Godhead. I may have supposed, however, in my naïve state, that possibly an angel, to be sure one who was quite a ways down the chain of command, might have been in the area and stopped in briefly to deliver either a Yea or a Nay. I'm being facetious, but the fact of the matter is that I was spiritually surprised, maybe even startled, that a matter of such eternal significance did not merit a more noteworthy divine reply.

To be sure, I have had ten thousand witnesses since then that God approved of the marriage between Shauna Sizemore and Robert Millet, and that he has blessed and sweetened that union during the decades. And now, as I look back on almost seventy years of life on this earth, after having passed through the satisfaction and sorrows, the delights and depression, the moments of unspeakable joy and the seasons of unrest, I am able to recognize clearly how the heavens were dealing with Shauna and me when we had fasted and prayed in 1970. I realize that my own spiritual expectations were unrealistic. What we felt on that cold morning almost fifty years ago was a settled conviction, a quiet awareness, a voice that was still and small, but one that would with the passing of time whisper through and pierce all things (see D&C 85:6). What we felt on that (for us) hallowed occasion was *peace*.

A Quiet Message from God

Some years ago, Elder Jay E. Jensen of the Seventy shared an experience and a significant lesson. He first observed that the Holy Ghost is vital in the work of the Lord, but sometimes the Saints are unaware of the many ways that the Spirit may direct us. He explained that while serving as a branch president in the Missionary Training Center, he heard a number of the missionaries remark that they did not have the kind of testimony they wished they had. Some even commented to the effect that they did not remember ever having a personal spiritual experience. Elder Jensen suggested that part of the problem might have been that these young people had read or heard about so many dramatic and sensational spiritual experiences in the past that they concluded that what they felt or experienced paled into insignificance.

"A number of years ago," he continued, "in a meeting of re-turned mission presidents, we reviewed different ways to improve missionaries' spirituality. One person said, 'We need to help all missionaries experience and recognize the burning of the bosom taught in Doctrine and Covenants 9:7–9.' A member of the First Quorum of the Seventy then shared the following experience:

"One of the Quorum of the Twelve came to tour the mission over which the Seventy was presiding. As they drove to the next zone conference, the Apostle turned to him and said, 'I wonder if you might have left an impression in the missionaries' minds that has created more problems than you can resolve. As I have traveled throughout the Church, I've found relatively few people who have experienced a burning of the bosom. In fact, I've had many people tell me that they've become frustrated because they have never experienced that feeling even though they have prayed or fasted for long periods of time.'

"He explained that Doctrine and Covenants 9:7–9 was given in response to the process of translating sacred records. There the burning of the bosom was appropriate. The principle can apply to personal revelation, he said, but more precisely it related to the translation of the Book of Mormon. He counseled the mission president to refer missionaries to other scriptural references about the Holy Ghost. For example, he cited the verse 'Did I not speak peace to your mind concerning the matter? What greater witness can you have than from God?' (D&C 6:23)."[1]

The context of that particular scriptural passage is worth understanding. In 1828 Joseph had yielded to the persuasions of Martin Harris and allowed the 116 pages of Book of Mormon manuscript (the book of Lehi) to pass out of his hands to Martin,

who made a solemn promise to show them only to his unbeliev-
ing wife and a specified number of people. Martin violated his
promise, the pages were subsequently lost, and the Lord withdrew
the plates, the Urim and Thummim, and His Holy Spirit from
Joseph for a season. Not long after, Oliver Cowdery began teaching school in Palmyra and for a time boarded with the Joseph
Smith Sr. family. While there, the family shared with him the
story of how Joseph Jr. had received direction from an angel to
begin the translation of an ancient scriptural record engraved
on golden plates. Oliver prayed about the matter and sought to
know if in fact it was of God. From the earliest history of the
Church (1832), we read the following from the Prophet: "The
plates were taken from me by the power of God and I was not
able to obtain them for a season. And it came to pass after much
humility and affliction of soul I obtained them again when [the]
*Lord appeared unto a young man by the name of Oliver Cowdery and
showed unto him the plates in a vision* and also the truth of the work
and what the Lord was about to do through me, his unworthy servant. Therefore [Oliver] was desirous to come and write for me."[2]
Oliver traveled to Harmony, Pennsylvania, arriving on 5 April
1829 and beginning his labor as a scribe on 7 April.

In that same month, a revelation was given to Joseph and
Oliver wherein the Savior commended Oliver "for what thou
hast done; for thou hast inquired of me, and behold, as often as
thou hast inquired thou hast received instruction of my Spirit.
If it had not been so, thou wouldst not have come to the place
where thou art at this time." This is fascinating. Here Oliver is
being told that it is no coincidence that he is now in Harmony,
with Joseph Smith, serving as a scribe, in a work that can only
be described as miraculous. Oliver had clearly been led along by
the Lord to where he is now. Then come these words: "Behold,
thou knowest that thou hast inquired of me and I did enlighten

thy mind; and now I tell thee these things that thou mayest know that thou hast been enlightened by the Spirit of truth" (D&C 6:14–15). It's as if Oliver is being told: "I'm giving you a revelation so that you may know that what you have been given in the past was revelation, divine guidance." Here a subsequent revelation confirms the reality and truthfulness of a former revelation.

Later in this revelation we note these words: "Verily, verily, I say unto you, if you desire a further witness, cast your mind upon the night that you cried unto me in your heart, that you might know concerning the truth of these things." And so in addition to the revelation now being given to him, if Oliver needed further assurance concerning the truth of this work, he should remember, think back upon the time when in the upstairs room of the Smith home, he had knelt and prayed, and the Lord had manifest powerfully to him that it was all true. Now this profound pronouncement: "*Did I not speak peace to your mind concerning the matter? What greater witness can you have than from God? And now, behold, you have received a witness; for if I have told you things which no man knoweth have you not received a witness?*" (D&C 6:22–24; emphasis added). Remember that, according to the 1832 history, the Savior appeared to Oliver and showed him a vision of the plates. Here the Lord teaches that the peace that had come to Oliver on that earlier occasion, the peace that accompanies the outpouring of God's Spirit, is every bit as spiritually impressive, as potent, as persuasive and convincing as a personal appearance or a vision.

Spiritual Expectations

Alma delivered an address to the people of Zarahemla, one in which he posed some forty questions of assessment, a kind of spiritual checklist. He came to the point where he desired to bear witness of what he had taught. We might ask ourselves, How did Alma know that he had in fact been called of God and that the work in which he was now engaged was heaven-approved? Many times I have asked that question in Book of Mormon classes at BYU. Generally, one of the first students to respond makes some reference to the fact that Alma and the sons of Mosiah had been struck down by an angel and had undergone a major conversion, much like Saul of Tarsus would experience some 120 years later.

Alma in fact tells us how he knew: "Do ye not suppose that I know of these things myself? Behold, I testify unto you that I do know that these things whereof I have spoken are true. And how do ye suppose I know of their surety? Behold, I say unto you they are made known unto me by the Holy Spirit of God. Behold, *I have fasted and prayed many days that I might know these things of myself.* And now I do know of myself that they are true; for *the Lord God hath made them manifest to me by his Holy Spirit*; and this is the spirit of revelation which is in me" (Alma 5:45–46; emphasis added). That's how Alma knew, and it's how you and I come to know. As our prophets have instructed us, the witness planted in the human soul by the power of the Holy Ghost is more indelible, more powerful even, than the appearance of heavenly beings.[3]

As members of The Church of Jesus Christ of Latter-day Saints, we are taught from the time we are children about Moses parting the Red Sea, about Gideon and his three hundred defeating a Philistine army of many thousands, about Joshua and the children of Israel bringing down the walls of Jericho. We learn of Jacob and Joseph and their prophetic dreams, of Elijah and Elisha raising the dead. And we bask in the light of the healing ministry of the Son of God and the signs and wonders wrought by his apostles after the Lord's crucifixion and resurrection. With the call of a modern prophet in 1820, the fulness of the gospel is restored, and as a pertinent part of that fulness, we see miracle upon miracle performed by the power of the Holy Priesthood. We read of visions of the Savior by special witnesses like Joseph Smith, Lorenzo Snow, Joseph F. Smith, Orson F. Whitney, and Melvin J. Ballard. Truly, to be a member of the Church of Jesus Christ is to be a member of the household of faith, and it is by faith that miracles are accomplished.

If there is a drawback, a concern about being awash as we are in the miraculous, it is that we may begin to take lightly or even ignore those marvelous miracles that are less visible, less fantastic, less sensational or dramatic. If there is a drawback, it is that the people of the covenant will "[look] beyond the mark" (Jacob 4:14), assume that if they are not seeing visions, entertaining angels, or enjoying the blessings of the Second Comforter, they must not be paying a sufficient price; their sacrifice is not sufficient or acceptable. And this would be tragic. When the apostle Paul addressed himself to the Corinthians, he pointed out that not all of the gifts of the Spirit are of equal spiritual value, and that some of the gifts, though less comely or attractive or enviable, are in fact among the most valuable. He encouraged the meridian Saints, for example, to seek earnestly to obtain the gift of prophecy, meaning the gift to speak the word of God by the gift and power of the Holy Spirit. He also commended those who had enjoyed the gift of tongues but warned them that such a gift had a limited utility and would probably do more to mystify and even repel those not of the faith than entice them (1 Corinthians 14).

Joseph the Prophet took a similar course. He noted that "there are only two gifts that could be made visible—the gift of tongues and the gift of prophecy. These are things that are the most talked about, and yet if a person spoke in an unknown tongue, according to Paul's testimony, he would be a barbarian to those present. They would say that it was gibberish."[4] He also provided sound and solid counsel to his people relative to the need to avoid the drama and sensationalism that we so often witness in our own Spirit-starved world: "The Lord cannot always be known by the thunder of His voice, by the display of His glory or by the manifestation of His power, and those that are the most anxious to see these things are the least prepared to meet [receive] them."⁵ As to spiritual gifts in the Church, the Prophet pointed out that "every Latter-day Saint had a gift, and by living a righteous life, and asking for it, the Holy Spirit would reveal it to him or her."⁶

One of the most important of all miracles is one that is usually enacted in private, during personal devotions, when a woman or a man is all alone with their God. It is a miracle that takes place throughout the entire planet, one that is enjoyed by millions, but one that is seldom seen by more than the recipient. That is the miracle that comes when a testimony of the gospel—or of a given gospel principle—is planted in the human heart. It is a gift from the Almighty, mediated by the third member of the Godhead. To acquire a spiritual conviction is to have been reborn. John the Beloved taught that "whosoever believeth that Jesus is the Christ is born of God: and every one that loveth him that begat [God] loveth him also that is begotten of him [the seeker after truth]" (1 John 5:1). To gain a testimony in this manner is to begin the process of conversion. President Harold B. Lee once explained that when a person is truly converted he "sees with his eyes what he ought to see; . . . he hears with his ears what he ought to hear; and . . . he understands with his heart what he ought to understand. And what he ought to see, hear, and understand is truth—eternal truth—and then practice it. That is conversion. . . . When we understand more than we know with our minds, when we understand with our hearts, then we know that the Spirit of the Lord is working upon us."⁷

"I Know"

My family and I first arrived in Tallahassee, Florida, where I was to oversee the Institute of Religion adjacent to Florida State University in 1977. We were quickly caught up in a marvelous community of Saints who loved the Lord and made living the gospel enjoyable, even fun. While our time was divided in several ways—being bishop of one of the wards, being a full-time doctoral student at FSU, teaching institute classes, and supervising six stakes of seminary—we did manage to develop some wonderful friendships, many of which are still very much precious and intact, nearly forty years later. One of my dearest friends was a man who with his family had joined the Church only a few years before we arrived there. His family proved to be a great asset to the ward, and the parents and children soon considered the Church to be a part of their extended family.

My friend, the father of this family (let's call him Rick) served for a time as my executive secretary, and so we grew even closer. I noticed that Rick bore his testimony quite often on fast Sunday, and in every case he would say, "I . . . (pause) *believe* God is our Heavenly Father, that Jesus is our Savior, that Joseph Smith is a prophet, and that the Book of Mormon is the word of God." Occasionally he would say something like this: "I cannot say that I *know* this work is true, but I do believe it." One night during the week and after interviews, we drove over to the local McDonalds for a quick bite to eat. We sat at the metal table outside the restaurant on what I think must have been a fall evening.

As we were finishing up, I turned to my friend and said, "Rick, I am always touched when I hear your testimony. Thank you for sharing it as you do. I'm sure that others in the ward are likewise strengthened by it." He became a bit emotional and expressed how very much the restored gospel meant to him and his family.

I looked him in the eye and asked, "Why don't you just break down and say, 'I *know* that God lives' or 'I *know* the restored gospel is true.' Why do you hesitate to use the word *know?*"

He sat up, looked me in the eye, and responded, "Bob, I've never seen God or Christ in this life. I wasn't in the Sacred Grove. I didn't watch as Joseph Smith translated the Book of Mormon. How can I say I know?"

We then had a worthwhile conversation about how spiritual things are known—by the power of the Spirit; how one does not need to have been an eyewitness of the resurrection to *know* that Jesus Christ lives today; to have been in the grove in Nauvoo when the Prophet Joseph preached, to *know,* by the power of the Holy Ghost, that God did call, prepare, and empower him.

As we have noted, Alma knew by that same power, as did the sons of Mosiah. The apostle Paul wrote that "*the things of God knoweth no man, except he has the Spirit of God.* Now, we have received, not the spirit of the world, but the Spirit which is of God; *that we might know* the things that are freely given to us of God. . . . For who hath known the mind of the Lord, that he may instruct him? But *we have the mind of Christ* (JST, 1 Corinthians 2:11–12, 16; emphasis added). Note the following passages:

"By the Spirit are *all things made known*" (1 Nephi 22:2; emphasis added).

"We also had many revelations, and the spirit of much prophecy; wherefore, we knew of Christ and his kingdom, which should come" (Jacob 1:6).

"Behold, great and marvelous are the works of the Lord. How unsearchable are the depths of the mysteries of him; and it is impossible that man should find out all his ways. And *no man knoweth* of his ways save it be revealed unto him" (Jacob 4:8; emphasis added).

"He that believeth these things which I have spoken, him will I visit with the manifestations of my Spirit, and *he shall know and bear record.* For because of my Spirit *he shall know* that these things are true; for it persuadeth men to do good" (Ether 4:11; emphasis added).

"And by the power of the Holy Ghost *ye may know* the truth of all things" (Moroni 10:5; emphasis added).

"Verily, verily, I say unto you, *I will impart unto you of my Spirit,* which shall enlighten your mind, which shall fill your soul with joy; and *then shall ye know, or by this shall you know,* all things whatsoever you desire of me, which are pertaining unto things of righteousness, in faith believing in me that you shall receive" (D&C 11:13–14; emphasis added).

"If thou shalt ask, thou shalt receive revelation upon revelation, *knowledge upon knowledge, that thou mayest know* the mysteries and peaceable things—that which bringeth joy, that which bringeth life eternal" (D&C 42:61; emphasis added).

"To some it is given by the Holy Ghost to know that Jesus Christ is the Son of God, and that he was crucified for the sins of the world" (D&C 46:13).

"Be still and know that I am God" (D&C 101:16).

To summarize, spiritual things may be *known* by the power of the Holy Ghost, and that knowledge is, in many ways, more convincing than anything that can be known through the five physical senses, by scientific analysis, or by empirical study. President Boyd K. Packer spoke of an experience he had on an airplane. His seatmate, an atheist, attempted to persuade him that there is no God. "'You are wrong,' I said, 'there is a God. I know he lives!'" The man, an attorney, demanded that Brother Packer tell him *how* he knew. As Brother Packer spoke of spirit, witness, prayer, discernment, or faith, the atheist declared that he had no idea what this religious leader was talking about.

At that point, the apostle asked the man if he knew what salt tastes like, to which the man said that obviously he did. "'Then,'

I said, 'assuming that I have never tasted salt, explain to me just what it tastes like.' After some thought, he ventured, 'Well—I—uh, it is not sweet, and it is not sour.' 'You've told me what it isn't, not what it is.'" After the attorney made a number of attempts to explain what salt tastes like and failed, Elder Packer said to him: "'I know there is a God. You ridiculed that testimony and said that if I *did* know, I would be able to tell you exactly *how* I know. My friend, spiritually speaking, I have tasted salt. I am no more able to convey to you in words how this knowledge has come than you are to tell me what salt tastes like. But I say to you again, there is a God! He does live! And just because you don't know, don't try to tell me that I don't know, for I do!'"[8]

Always Remember

There is a remarkable story in Mosiah 18 in the Book of Mormon. Alma the Elder had been deeply moved by the final words of Abinadi the prophet in his warning and testimony delivered to king Noah and his wicked priests. The account indicates that Alma "repented of his sins and iniquities, and went about privately among the people, and began to teach the words of Abinadi," including the eternal significance of the sufferings and death, the atonement and resurrection of Christ, the coming Messiah. Many of the people who listened to Alma were converted to the message of the gospel of Jesus Christ.

"And it came to pass that as many as did believe him did go forth to a place which was called Mormon. . . . Now, there was in Mormon a fountain of pure water, and Alma resorted thither, there being near the water a thicket of small trees, where he did hide himself in the daytime from the searches of the king." Alma began to baptize these people in the waters of Mormon, and this group became a church in the wilderness, "the church of Christ," one of the first of its kind in the Nephite record (Mosiah 18:1–13,

16–17). Alma organized the church, ordained priests to teach the people, generated a spirit of love and cooperation among the new members of the church, and taught them to "impart of their substance, every one according to that which he had . . . of their own free will." Alma's converts "did walk uprightly before God, imparting to one another both temporally and spiritually according to their needs and their wants" (Mosiah 18:17–29).

What then follows in the scriptural account is this tender verse: "And now it came to pass that all this was done in Mormon, yea, by the waters of Mormon, . . . *how beautiful are they to the eyes of them who there came to the knowledge of their Redeemer*; yea, and how blessed are they, for *they shall sing to his praise forever*" (Mosiah 18:30; emphasis added). These marvelous people would never forget what had taken place that day. They would always remember what they felt, what they experienced. And they would never forget the waters of Mormon, this singular spot of ground that became hallowed to those who entered into the gospel covenant.

Many years ago I traveled with my son to Louisiana to visit my family and friends. This part of the country is where I grew up, where I first went to church, where I was baptized, received the Aaronic and Melchizedek Priesthoods, and left on a mission. Having been in the area for over a week, and as our time in the Baton Rouge area was finished, we drove north to the community of Baker to a nice multiphase LDS meetinghouse. We left the car, and he and I walked closer to the church. My son turned and looked at me. "Why are we here?" he inquired. I then began to tell my story. I spoke of how when our small branch began to gather in this community, this particular spot of ground was a large swamp. I told him of the chicken dinners, the spaghetti dinners, the doughnut sales, the bazaars, even the rodeo we sponsored, all to raise funds to build the first phase of a building, basically a classroom facility. We walked over to the white block building and I pointed out that I was one of many who had painted those walls, inside and out.

I described how we then began a whole series of new fund raisers to be able to build the next phase, a beautiful chapel. I told him of how tough it was for a small group of us to lift those huge beams that supported the roof. I rolled my right pants leg up and showed him a scar. I explained that that scar had been a cut that resulted from sliding down that extremely steep roof and snagging my leg on a nail. This was where I bore my testimony for the first time, I explained. This was the place where my dad had served as the first bishop of the ward and the site where I was taught the gospel by devoted members, simple members, uneducated by the world's standards but highly schooled in the things of the Spirit. It was in that chapel that I delivered my farewell address before leaving on a mission. I remember saying the following to my son: "There is a part of me in that church building. And there is a big part of that building that is in me." I thought to myself: "A very significant part of my testimony of the restored gospel resides in my soul because I invested myself in that building and, more particularly, in what took place *in that building*. How beautiful this spot of earth has become to me!" There's a good reason why I always drive north to this spot each time I travel south to visit family. This is hallowed ground. Memory is a vital aspect of a testimony of the gospel.

On the other hand, when a person's faith is shaken, when doubts surface and the mind becomes clouded, it is so easy to begin to ask oneself, "Do I really know? How do I know? Was what I felt then real? Was it a message from God, or was it instead some kind of self-fulfilling desire to believe?" Unless the person is able to escape or push beyond such doubts, he or she may very well succumb to what I call "spiritual amnesia." There is a reason why the scriptures and the prophets continue to plead with the children of God to *remember*. Elder Marlin K. Jensen of the Seventy observed that "if we pay close attention to the uses of the word *remember* in the holy scriptures, we will recognize that remembering in the way God intends is a fundamental and saving principle of the gospel. This is so because prophetic admonitions to remember are frequently calls to action: to listen, to see, to do, to obey, to repent. When we remember in God's way, we overcome our human tendency simply to gird for the battle of life and actually engage in the battle itself, doing all in our power to resist temptation and avoid sinning."[9]

What I have noticed, time and again, is that Latter-day Saints who cannot seem to find answers to their tough questions or relief from their vexations of the soul, who then begin to wonder whether it's worth it to remain in the faith, also begin to look back with a kind of mental myopia. That is, they start the process, a deadly process at that, of reinterpreting their past. Terryl and Fiona Givens wrote: "We tend to reinterpret the past *on the basis of the present. We are creatures of the moment*, so, rather than remember, we reconstruct what once we knew in the light of present uncertainty or loss, which can all too easily overwhelm what we once held as true and real. All too often we forget the gentle impressions we felt, the calm soothing of troubled hearts and minds, or even greater manifestations of divine love."[10]

In speaking to students at Brigham Young University, Elder Jeffrey R. Holland made a significant request, a plea really, with these young people, that applies to every baptized member of the Church. "I wish to encourage every one of us," he said, "regarding the opposition that so often comes after enlightened decisions have been made, after moments of revelation and conviction have given us a peace and an assurance we thought we would never lose." He then quoted from Hebrews: "Cast not away therefore your confidence, which hath great recompense of re-ward. For ye have need of patience, that, after ye have done the will of God, ye might receive the promise" (Hebrews 10:35–36). Elder Holland continued: "In Latter-day Saint talk that is to say, Sure it is tough—before you join the Church, while you are trying to join, and after you have joined. That is the way it has always been, Paul says, but don't draw back. *Don't panic and retreat. Don't lose your confidence. Don't forget how you once felt. Don't distrust the experience you had. . . .* Once there has been illumination, beware the temptation to retreat from a good thing. *If it was right when you prayed about it and trusted it and lived for it, it is right now.*"[11]

Conclusion

A visionary experience that President Brigham Young had al-most three years following the death of Joseph Smith seems espe-cially relevant. Brother Brigham said, "Joseph stepped toward me and looking very earnestly, yet pleasantly, said, 'Tell the people to be humble and faithful and be sure to keep the Spirit of the Lord and it will lead them right. Be careful and not turn away the still small voice; it will teach [them] what to do and where to go; it will yield the fruits of the kingdom. Tell the brethren to keep their hearts open to conviction, so that when the Holy Ghost comes to them, their hearts will be ready to receive it. They can tell the Spirit of the Lord from all other spirits. It will whisper peace and joy to their souls and it will take malice, hatred, envy-ing, strife, and all evil from their hearts; and their whole desire will be to do good, bring forth righteousness, and build up the kingdom of God. Tell the brethren if they will follow the Spirit of the Lord they will go right.'"[12]

The longer I live, the more clearly I see how crucial it is for a member of the Church to live in such a manner as to keep that precious gift of the Holy Ghost working in our lives. When the

Spirit is present, we see things as they really are. When the Spirit is guiding us, we pursue paths that are in our eternal best interest. And when the Spirit of God finds lodgment within our soul, our memory of spiritual "red letter days" is crisp and sharp—how we came to faith, what it felt like when we gained a testimony, the sweet delight we knew when with us it was "the kingdom of God or nothing," the moments and events of the past that reinforced and sustained that conviction. The influence that flows from the third member of the Godhead leads us to do good, to act justly, to walk humbly, to judge righteously; that Spirit also enlightens our minds and fills our souls with joy (D&C 11:12–13). President Ezra Taft Benson perhaps said it best when he observed that "this latter-day work is spiritual. It takes spirituality to comprehend it, to love it, and to discern it. Therefore, we should seek the Spirit in all we do. That is our challenge."[13]

I once heard Stephen R. Covey say in a BYU devotional: "I believe sometimes that as Latter-day Saints we are like fish who discover water last. We are so immersed in the element that we are unaware of its presence. We have been immersed in the revelations of the Lord in this dispensation. No dispensation can compare to this one. . . . In a sense, this is a dispensation of the Holy Ghost." Brother Covey then reminded students that "it's possible to be given a gift and receive not that gift."[14] Indeed, what greater witness can you and I have than the peace and joy and sense of commitment and devotion to the gospel cause that comes quietly but powerfully to each of us who have been baptized and confirmed? That we will always remember what we once *felt*, what we once *resolved*, what we once *believed*, and yes, what we once *knew*, is my hope and prayer.

Chapter 11

"LORD, TO WHOM SHALL WE GO?"

Perhaps someone reading this book is contemplating making a significant change in their religious life, maybe even disassociating from The Church of Jesus Christ of Latter-day Saints. Surely no one would make a decision of this spiritual magnitude without an immense amount of careful, ponderous, even prayerful thinking. One must, as the Savior taught us, count the cost (see Luke 14:28). That cost reaches well beyond personal discomfort and distress, for the influence of Mormonism reaches to family, friends, and culture.

What Else Is There?

Not long after I joined the BYU Religious Education faculty I attended a conference where presentations on Mormonism were made, some of which took issue with a number of the Church's positions on social and family matters. One presentation had to do with what the speaker called "the unrighteous dominion of a stifling Church hierarchy." Later that morning I attended a workshop on doctrinal matters that was actually quite insightful, and the participants didn't seem to be pushing any particular agenda. Another session focused on events in Church history that reflected "unchristian behavior" of nineteenth-century Latter-day

Saints. An evening presentation I attended was more like a pep rally than anything else; the speaker seemed to be attempting to rally forces against the Church and its leaders.

The second day I returned to the conference, wondering what might unfold. One man, a convert to the Church, spent the first two thirds of his talk quipping about all of the silly, nonsensical, embarrassing, and even bizarre things that had happened to him since becoming a Latter-day Saint. The audience laughed and applauded and nodded their heads in agreement. And then the speaker became very sober and said, in essence: "There really are some dumb and painful things that happen within Mormon culture." He summarized by noting that there are matters that for him just don't add up, insensitive remarks and behaviors that really sting, and recurring situations that need to be corrected.

After a short pause, he said something like the following: "But now let's get to the meat of the matter: I have spent many years of my life studying religion, investigating Christian and non-Christian faiths, engaging their literature and participating in their worship." He indicated that he had seen it all, from top to bottom and from back to front. And then he said, essentially: "Guess what: there's nothing in the religious world that will provide near as much eternal perspective or satisfy your soul, that comes even close to what the LDS Church can do for a person. This is all there is. If there is a true church, this is it, with its warts and all." He then advised attenders to get comfortable with what they have. "There's nothing any better out there. I assure you of that."

That evening as I drove home I reflected on the two days I had spent at the conference. It reminded me of a very tender scene in the New Testament, an episode mentioned earlier. Jesus had just delivered the Bread of Life Sermon, a deep and penetrating message on the vital importance of partaking fully of the Person and powers of the Messiah. Many in the crowd at Capernaum were perplexed and even offended, especially when the Savior taught: "I am the living bread which came down from heaven: if any man eat of this bread, he shall live for ever: and the bread that I will give is my flesh, which I will give for the life of the world. . . . Except ye eat the flesh of the Son of man, and drink his blood, ye have no life in you. Whoso eateth my flesh, and drinketh my blood, hath eternal life; and I will raise him up at the last day" (John 6:51, 53–54). The result: "From that time many of his disciples went back," John records, "and walked no more with him. Then said Jesus unto the twelve, Will ye also go away?"

What a poignant moment. Our Lord seems to display a sense of disappointment, a somber sadness for those in the darkness who cannot comprehend the Light. Is the price too much to pay? Is the cost of discipleship so great that even those closest to him will leave the apostolic fellowship? "Then Simon Peter answered him, *Lord, to whom shall we go? thou hast the words of eternal life.* And we believe and are sure that thou art that Christ, the Son of the living God" (John 6:66–69; emphasis added). Once a genuine and earnest truth seeker has enjoyed sweet fellowship with the Christ, how does he or she turn away? Where do you go? What possible message, way of life, social interactions, or eternal promise can even compare with what Jesus offers?

Where would the apostles go if they chose to forsake their calling and travel other paths? Would they revert to Judaism? Would they stay in Jerusalem or return to their homes in Galilee? Would they spend more time in the synagogues, listening to the teachings of noted rabbis? Would they join the zealots and battle the Roman overlords? Who will give to them the satisfaction, the sustenance, the intellectual stimulation, who will light a fire in their souls like Jesus of Nazareth?

Hard to Leave Behind

I have been rather fascinated to notice that a surprising number of persons who leave The Church of Jesus Christ of Latter-day Saints do not choose to attend a different church or synagogue or mosque. They do not elect to become Roman Catholic or Presbyterian or Evangelical or Eastern Orthodox or Jewish or Muslim. One person who had become disassociated with the Church wrote to me: "Like a lot of people who leave, I transitioned fairly quickly to an Agnostic [one who does not really know whether there is a God]. I had had too many spiritual experiences in my life to deny some kind of higher power existed and [so I] was unable to make the leap to Atheism."

Why would this be the case? I suppose one could never be completely sure (and certainly each person who leaves may have a very different reason), but I have a hunch. From the time little children begin to attend Primary to the time they arrive at the twilight of their life, they are encouraged, even charged to pray, to pray often, to pray regularly and earnestly. They are told how important it is to gain a testimony of the gospel of Jesus Christ for themselves, and it is explained hundreds of times during their lives that such a conviction can come only through the work of the Holy Spirit, only as they pray and ask God for a witness. And that spiritual assurance does come. Once persons seek for and obtain a testimony, they then continue to pray and fast and serve and labor to acquire a deeper and more abiding faith, one that cannot be "tossed to and fro, and carried about with every wind of doctrine" (Ephesians 4:14); they strive to obtain a conviction that is firm and unshakable.

I think I can picture that person sitting alone and reflecting on what he or she is leaving behind and where they might go. I can visualize such people saying to themselves, "If this isn't it, if the way of the Latter-day Saints is not God's way, then I have serious doubts that His way is out there." Consequently they either drift into the ranks of the less active, or in some cases, ask that their names be removed from the records of the Church. And some of them feel no compulsion, no motivation to attend other churches or affiliate with other denominations.

On a few occasions I have had acquaintances who have chosen to leave the Church vow to me that they had no intention whatsoever to become an enemy of the faith they once embraced. One man said it this way: "I just need a break from religion. I no longer believe in the LDS faith, but I am prepared to go my way without causing problems for the Church." It's a fine thing if a person who has become embittered with the Church is able to leave it without that embitterment beginning to spill over into their post-church life. But it's a real risk.

A man by the name of Isaac Behunin once stated to the Prophet Joseph Smith: "If I should leave this Church, I would not do as those men [who had become angry apostates] have done. I would go to some remote place where Mormonism had never been heard of, settle down, and no one would ever learn I knew anything about it." Joseph's response should serve as a warning to any and all of us: "Brother Behunin, you don't know what you would do. No doubt these men once thought as you do. Before you joined this Church you stood on neutral ground. When the gospel was preached, good and evil were set before you. You could choose either or neither. There were two opposite masters inviting you to serve them. *When you joined this Church you enlisted to serve God. When you did that, you left the neutral ground,* and you never can get back on to it. Should you forsake the Master you enlisted to serve, it will be by the instigation of the evil one, and you will follow his dictation and be his servant."[1]

To me one of the saddest of all scenarios is the man or woman who once possessed a firm and vibrant testimony of the restored gospel, who represented so well the best of Mormonism, who has, for one reason or another, chosen to turn away from a faith and way of life that had brought so very much happiness to them in years past. This picture is sad enough, to be sure, but even more painful is the person who leaves and then feels compelled to fight that faith tooth and nail. Elder Neal A. Maxwell described the spiritual warfare this way: "Church members will live in this wheat-and-tares situation until the Millennium. Some real tares even masquerade as wheat, including the few eager individuals who lecture the rest of us about Church doctrines in which they no longer believe. They criticize the use of Church resources to which they no longer contribute. They condescendingly seek to counsel the Brethren whom they no longer sustain. Confrontive, except of themselves, of course, they leave the Church, but they cannot leave the Church alone."[2]

I have been asked many times by religious scholars or church leaders of other faiths this question: "Bob, what would you do if you were not LDS? What faith, what church or denomination would you pursue?" I have always responded honestly—that I probably would not join or affiliate with any other religious group, Christian or non-Christian. I say that as one who is not completely unaware of the tremendous good these religious institutions do and the truth they possess and proclaim. Stated simply, it would be very difficult to undo, discount, or dismiss a lifetime of volunteer service, worship, temple attendance, thousands of hours of study in the scripture and the teachings of living prophets.

An Experiment in Faith

Blaise Pascal (1623–1662) was a French mathematician, physicist, and philosopher. One of the products of his amazingly creative life was what has come to be known as Pascal's Wager, his own defense of the Christian faith. He observed, quite correctly, that either Christianity is true or it is not. Either Jesus of Nazareth was the Son of the Living God, or he was not. Either Jesus performed miracles, suffered, bled, and died on the cross to atone for the sins of all humanity, or he did not. Either Jesus rose from the dead into glorious immortality three days after his death, or he did not. Either life within the Christian fold brings the greatest measure of happiness here and opens one to heaven hereafter, or it does not. It's really that simple. There are no half measures that will do.

Think for a moment. What if a person embraced a profligate lifestyle, used and abused other people all his days, and spent his earthly resources on wine, women, and song, when in fact Christianity was true, the one sure path to a closer relationship with Deity? He would die and eventually learn that his earthly existence had largely been wasted, that he had forfeited his opportunity to be with God in heaven.

Pascal posed a second question: What if a man accepted Christianity, lived his life in conformity with the teachings and example of Jesus, and died firm in the faith, when in fact Christianity was not true, that there really was, for example, no life after death, no immortality of the soul? Pascal inquired about "what harm will come to you from taking this course [committing fully to Christianity]? You will be faithful, honest, humble, grateful, doing good, a sincere and true friend. It is, of course, true [that] you will not take part in corrupt pleasure, in glory, in the pleasures of high living. But will you not have other [pleasures and delights]? I tell you that you will win thereby in this life."[3]

Psychologist and philosopher William James (1842–1910) agreed with Pascal. He taught that religion results in "a new zest which adds itself like a gift to life, and takes the form either of lyrical enchantment or of appeal to earnestness and heroism. . . .

An assurance of safety and a temper of peace, and, in relation to others, a preponderance of loving affections."[4]

Christian theologian Alister McGrath wrote: "Faith is basically the resolve to live our lives on the assumption that certain things are true and trustworthy, in the confident assurance that they *are* true and trustworthy. And that one day we will know with absolute certainty that they are true and trustworthy."[5] Samuel Shoemaker commented that the advice he often gives to people who are wrestling with doubt is simply this: *act as if*. "Act as if the whole thing, the gospel, the Good News, the reality and love of God as revealed by Christ—act as if it were all true. Never mind if you have doubts, never mind if you feel it's all too good to be true. *Act as if it were so. Behave as if you believed! This isn't self-deception; it's just another spiritual experiment*. And it may well have verifiable results.

"*Tell the doubters and shaky ones to try the way of believing as against the way of not believing*. If they do try, and stick to it, more and more they'll find themselves being swept along by a current not of their own making. Their level of faith will begin to rise, because the faculty of faith grows stronger with use, and by acting as if they'll have been using it!"[6]

As we discussed earlier in this work, Jesus himself encouraged people to follow his counsel, forsake their sins, and come unto him for happiness here and eternal life hereafter. The formula was simple—DO and then KNOW whether the gospel he preached was something he had conjured up or was, in reality, the one and only way to the Father, to salvation (John 7:16–17; 14:6). So it is with Mormonism: live it and see. Practice its principles and receive its covenants and ordinances and observe how it works upon the soul. "Prove all things," the apostle Paul charged the former-day Saints; "hold fast that which is good" (1 Thessalonians 5:21).

A Faith Worth Fighting For

My sincere recommendation to someone wavering in the faith is to take the time and expend the effort to re-kindle the flame of faith that they spent in gaining a witness in the first place and maintaining it through the years. If you once came to know the message is true by the power of the Spirit, have you spent as much time on your knees recently, as you did then? Have you been direct, specific, and earnest in your pleadings to the same God? Do your spiritual efforts match your mental gymnastics? If it's fair game to question what you once knew to be true, it's more than fair to question your questions or doubt your doubts. I don't think I have ever met a person who chose to leave The Church of Jesus Christ of Latter-day Saints whose explanation for leaving was that they had prayed about the matter and received divine direction to do so. There must be people out there who can make that claim, but I haven't met them yet.

From my perspective, to doubt our doubts is to be courageous rather than cavalier when it comes to eternal things. We cannot, for example, afford to be casual in our doubting of doubts and thus succumb to spiritual and intellectual laziness. In other words, no one of us should ever allow a doubt to reign when in fact it has not won that lofty perch through proving itself *beyond all doubt*. Just as for me it takes too much faith to be an atheist— to witness, for example, the order and precision of the cosmos or the complexity of the human body and still hold to an atheistic posture—so we should not be so kindly, such a pushover, as to allow our faith system to go by the way without intellectual and spiritual kicking and screaming on our part.

Our Father in heaven knows all things, *including what he has made known to you and me*. We cannot and must not treat such knowledge lightly or abandon it carelessly. Our duty as disciples is to "stir up the gift of God, which is in [us]. . . . For God hath not given us the spirit of fear; but of power, and of love, and of a sound mind. Be not thou therefore ashamed of the testimony of our Lord" (2 Timothy 1:6–8). To quote Jude, the brother of Jesus, we must "earnestly contend for the faith which was once delivered" to you and me (Jude 1:3). Truly, our faith is worth fighting for.

I mentioned earlier in this work that our family had left our relatively strong ward in Baton Rouge, Louisiana, and relocated to Baker, several miles to the north. We joined the tiny branch there just before I was to begin the ninth grade at a new school. Our family did so after a period of relative inactivity, about three years. Our first day at the new church (held, as I mentioned, in the girl's gymnasium at the high school) is memorable to me. While I did not know many of the young people, I felt warmth in their welcomes, and I felt the Spirit of the Lord as we sang the same hymns and took the same Sacrament of the Lord's Supper that I had remembered. From my point of view, it was a glorious day; our absence from church had been extremely painful for me.

I found out later in the day that not all members of our family had been extended the same kindness as I had. After we arrived home from church and as I was changing clothes, I overheard Mom and Dad talking (their bedroom was right across the hall from mine). Then I heard something I had only witnessed a time or two in all my young years: I heard my dad weeping. I moved closer to my door and tried to see what the problem was. I heard Mom say, "Lou, what's the matter?"

Dad answered, "They won't even give me a chance."

"What are you talking about?" Mom asked.

Dad explained that as we first entered the gym that morning, a member of the branch, an old acquaintance of my dad's family, approached Dad and said quite loudly, "Well, my goodness. You decided to come to church? I think the walls might fall down!"

At that second I almost felt guilty for having been welcomed as I was when I heard Dad's distress. Mom embraced him and tried to reassure him. Then after a moment and after he had composed himself, I heard my wonderful father utter these exact words, timeless words that I will remember as long as I live: "But you know what? This is my church, too, and ain't no man gonna chase me out of my church!"

It would be hard for me to count the number of times I have been required to lean on that bold declaration of my father. Why? Simply because it is inevitable that many, many times through our years of Church membership, you and I will be bumped and bruised, insulted and misunderstood by members of the Church who were insensitive or perhaps even cruel. Elder Neal A. Maxwell, on many occasions, spoke of how our associations and interactions with other members of the Lord's Christian community is a significant part of developing Christian character; we serve as one another's "clinical material."[7] And just at that point when my thoughts descend to, "Well, I'll show them—I'll never come back to this church," I hear Dad's voice and remember, importantly, that this is my Church, too, and no person, man or woman, boy or girl, will force me out.

"Brothers and sisters, this is a divine work in process," Elder Jeffrey R. Holland reminded us, "with the manifestations and blessings of it abounding in every direction, so please don't hyperventilate if from time to time issues arise that need to be examined, understood, and resolved. They do and they will. *In this Church, what we know will always trump what we do not know. And remember, in this world, everyone is to walk by faith.*

"So be kind regarding human frailty—your own as well as that of those who serve with you in a Church led by volunteer, mortal men and women. Except in the case of His only perfect Begotten Son, imperfect people are all God has ever had to work with. That must be terribly frustrating to Him, but He deals with it. So should we. And when you see imperfection, remember that the limitation is *not* in the divinity of the work."[8]

A Crucial Decision

One of the joys of my life in the last two decades has been the sweet but challenging opportunity (a privilege, really) to come to know men and women of other faiths, professors and ministers really. We have spoken deeply on doctrinal matters, sung together, prayed together, eaten together, even mourned together the passing of colleagues. One of my beloved associates of another faith asked recently how I felt about all of the negative attention the Church was receiving these days and, more particularly, to what extent my faith was being tested by attacks on the First Vision, the Book of Mormon, the book of Abraham, plural marriage, or the character of Joseph Smith.

He asked, "Bob, doesn't some of this stuff trouble you? Has it ever occurred to you that you have given your life, personal and professional, to a lie, a hoax?"

"No, not at all," I replied. "I'm very persuaded that it is all true."

His next query: "Given all the sensitive and troublesome issues you folks are facing, wouldn't it be easier for you to renounce it all and shift your allegiance elsewhere?"

I indicated that I was perfectly happy with my faith and way of life and felt confident that solid answers are now available or will eventually come.

As I flew home from our group dialogue, I thought back on that conversation. I recalled words by Elder Neil L. Andersen in general conference. When I arrived home, I found the specific talk and reviewed it. The part that stood out to me was the following:

"The cause in which we are laboring is true. We respect the beliefs of our friends and neighbors. We are all sons and daughters of God. We can learn much from other men and women of faith and goodness. . . .

"Yet we know that Jesus is the Christ. He is resurrected. In our day, through the Prophet Joseph Smith, the priesthood of God has been restored. We have the gift of the Holy Ghost. The Book of Mormon is what we claim it to be. The promises of the temple are certain. . . . It's true, isn't it? Then what else matters?"

The words of Elder Andersen that have changed my life and assisted me in my quest to know why I am not derailed by otherwise troublesome matters are these: "*Faith is not only a feeling; it is a decision.* With prayer, study, obedience, and covenants, we build and fortify our faith. *Our conviction of the Savior and His latter-day work becomes the powerful lens through which we judge all else.* Then, as we find ourselves in the crucible of life, . . . we have the strength to take the right course."[9] Faith is a DECISION. What I know to be true motivates, even impels me to live out my faith, to uphold and defend that faith, to dedicate myself fully and completely to the establishment of Zion and the building of the kingdom of God.

In a subsequent general conference, Elder Andersen said: "Faith in the Lord Jesus Christ is not something ethereal, floating loosely in the air. Faith does not fall upon us by chance or stay with us by birthright. *Faith in Jesus Christ is a gift from heaven that comes as we choose to believe and as we seek it and hold on to it.* Your faith is either growing stronger or becoming weaker. . . . The future of your faith is not by chance, but by choice."[10] If we now go back to where this book began, let me re-ask the question that is the title of this volume: "Whatever happened to faith?" Whatever happened to people's abilities to stay calm, breathe deeply, and continue to believe and obey while the search for answers or solutions is under way? Whatever happened to the rather simple choice to assume the best, rather than the worst, about our

Church, its scriptures, and its prophet-leaders? Whatever happened to the resolution and decision that our pioneer forebears made to stay aboard the Good Ship Zion until it docks in the celestial harbor? Elder Andersen continued: *"Faith never demands an answer to every question but seeks the assurance and courage to move forward, sometimes acknowledging, 'I don't know everything, but I do know enough to continue on the path of discipleship.'"*[11]

Conclusion

There are just too many things about The Church of Jesus Christ of Latter-day Saints that bring joy and peace and even excitement to my heart, light and knowledge to my mind, for me to choose to throw it all away because I am uncertain or unsettled about this or that issue. For me, when it comes to the Church and the restored gospel, *the whole is much, much greater than the sum of its parts.* If you or one you love is contemplating leaving the Church: Hold on. Don't rush into this. Please count the cost. I am fully persuaded that there is far more to gain than there is to lose by remaining a practicing, believing Latter-day Saint.

What if you are not sure you believe it all? That's okay, since we are all at different levels of conviction and testimony. You may bristle at one thing that causes me absolutely no concern, but I may stay up nights ruminating on an issue that was settled in your heart years ago. As Elder Holland put it, this work in which we are engaged is a work in progress, as is each son or daughter of God both within and outside The Church of Jesus Christ of Latter-day Saints. Decades ago I heard a story of a father expressing disappointment to a child over a matter that at the moment seemed to dad to be quite serious. Teary eyed, the young teenager looked his dad in the eyes and said, "Dad, please don't give up on me. Heavenly Father isn't finished with me yet." And so it is with each of us. Thank God for His patience and understanding, for His willingness to continue to work on us and with us.

The restored Church seems now to be passing through some "close places," as Heber C. Kimball prophesied. This is not like any day that I have ever known. Truly, the Savior warned that "all things shall be in commotion; and surely, men's hearts shall fail them" (D&C 88:91; compare 45:26). The way along the gospel path is narrow, for some an extremely tight squeeze, just as the Savior explained it would be (Matthew 7:13–14; 3 Nephi 14:13–14). It is clear to me that this is also a time of great sifting. Elder Neal A. Maxwell warned prophetically that "much sifting will occur because of lapses in righteous behavior which go unrepented of. A few will give up instead of holding out to the end. A few will be deceived by defectors. Likewise, others will be offended, for sufficient unto each dispensation are the stumbling blocks thereof."[12]

This is, nonetheless, the path that leads to life eternal (Matthew 7:13–14; 3 Nephi 14:13–14). Every member of the Church who refuses to yield to cynicism; who turns a deaf ear to the naysayers; who decides to hold on, be patient, and exercise faith; who commits to "search diligently, pray always, and be believing," learns in time and through quiet but satisfying experience that "all things shall work together for [their] good" (D&C 90:24). Those who follow such a course thereby position themselves to hear the voice of the Lord whisper reassuringly and from time to time, "This is the way, walk ye in it" (Isaiah 30:21).

NOTES

EPIGRAPH

Joseph Smith, 235.

PREFACE

1. *Teachings of Thomas S. Monson*, 108.
2. *Teachings of Thomas S. Monson*, 111.

CHAPTER 1: THE SIFTING HAS BEGUN

1. Whitney, *Life of Heber C. Kimball*, 446; emphasis added.
2. Whitney, *Life of Heber C. Kimball*, 449–50; emphasis added.
3. *New Shorter Oxford English Dictionary*, s.v. "sift."
4. *Random House College Dictionary*, s.v. "halt."
5. McConkie, *Doctrinal New Testament Commentary*, 1:361–62.
6. *Teachings of George Albert Smith*, 27; emphasis added.
7. *Hymns*, no. 255.
8. *Brigham Young*, 82–83.

CHAPTER 2: EXAMINE YOURSELVES

1. *Teachings of Howard W. Hunter*, 236.
2. *Teachings of Howard W. Hunter*, 238; emphasis added.
3. Uchtdorf, "It Works Wonderfully!" *Ensign*, Nov. 2015, 21.
4. Clayton, "Rooted in Christ," *Ensign*, Aug. 2016, 21; emphasis added.
5. See Packer, *That All May Be Edified*, 117–18.
6. *Howard W. Hunter*, 270–71.
7. *Hymns*, no. 19.
8. Rasband, "Standing with the Leaders of the Church," *Ensign*, May 2016, 47; emphasis added.
9. Kimball, "Listen to the Prophets," *Ensign*, May 1978, 77; emphasis added.
10. Eyring, "Eyes to See, Ears to Hear."

11. Roberts, *Life of John Taylor*, 39–40; emphasis added; see also Givens and Grow, *Parley P. Pratt*, 101.
12. *Joseph Smith*, 72.
13. *Words of Joseph Smith*, 7; punctuation modernized.
14. See Smith, *Gospel Doctrine*, 58, 126.

CHAPTER 3: THE DARK VEIL OF UNBELIEF

1. Webster, *American Dictionary of the English Language*, s.v. "doubt."
2. *Lectures on Faith*, 46; emphasis added.
3. *Lectures on Faith*, 52; emphasis added; see also 71.
4. Mohler, *Atheism Remix*, 18–19; emphasis added.
5. *Teachings of Harold B. Lee*, 88.
6. Widtsoe, *Evidences and Reconciliations*, 31–32; emphasis added.
7. Nash, "Guided Safely Home."
8. In Lee, *Stand Ye in Holy Places*, 57; emphasis added.
9. McConkie, *Promised Messiah*, xvii.
10. See Kolodiejchuk, *Mother Teresa*.
11. Mason, *Planted*, 19.
12. Ballard, "Opportunities and Responsibilities of CES Teachers."
13. See Smith, *Doctrines of Salvation*, 3:1.
14. Maxwell, *Not My Will, but Thine*, 35.

CHAPTER 4: HOW DID WE GET HERE?

1. Gabriel Vahanian, in *Death of God Debate*, 16.
2. Carter, *Culture of Disbelief*, 6–7, 13 (ellipses in original), 23.
3. Maxwell, *Notwithstanding My Weakness*, 45.
4. McDowell and Hostetler, *Right from Wrong*, 12–13; see also Wilson, *Moral Sense*, 5, 9.
5. Robinson, *Honest to God*, 109; see also Fletcher, *Situation Ethics*, chapters 1 and 2.
6. See Carlos E. Asay, "Salt of the Earth," *Ensign*, May 1980, 42.
7. Wilson, *Moral Sense*, 10.
8. MacArthur, *Vanishing Conscience*, 21.
9. MacArthur, *Vanishing Conscience*, 22–23.
10. Penrose, in Conference Report, Oct. 1911, 48.
11. McDowell and Hostetler, *Right from Wrong*, 78.
12. Lewis, *Mere Christianity*, 54; emphasis added.
13. Maxwell, *Not My Will, but Thine*, 9.
14. A powerful message that teaches us the "why" behind the commandment to stay morally clean is in Holland and Holland, *On Earth As It Is in Heaven*, 182–97.
15. Packer, "Great Plan of Happiness."
16. Packer, "Little Children," *Ensign*, Nov. 1986, 17.
17. *Random House College Dictionary*, s.v. "secular."
18. Mohler, *Atheism Remix*, 36–37.
19. Maxwell, *Not My Will, but Thine*, 38.
20. Mohler, *Atheism Remix*, 12, 13.

21. In *Christian Century* 133, no. 22 (26 Oct. 2016): 16–17.

22. See Smith and Denton, *Soul Searching*, 162–70. See also Creasy-Dean, *Almost Christian*, a study on youth and religion that illustrates how the beliefs of teenagers mirror what they are taught at church.

Chapter 5: Why People Leave

1. Uchtdorf, "Come, Join with Us," *Ensign*, Nov. 2013, 22.

2. Hinckley, "Find the Lambs, Feed the Sheep," *Ensign*, May 1999, 108.

3. Mason, *Planted*, 77, 79; paragraphing altered.

4. Erekson, "Understanding Church History by Study and Faith," *Ensign*, Feb. 2017, 57.

5. See Jorgensen, "Mantle of the Prophet Joseph," in *Opening the Heavens*, 373–407.

6. *Joseph Smith*, 207.

7. McKay, in Conference Report, Apr. 1907, 11; see also Apr. 1962, 7.

8. Christofferson, "The Doctrine of Christ," *Ensign*, May 2012, 88.

9. McConkie, "Gathering of Israel and the Return of Christ," 3, 5.

10. Erekson, "Understanding Church History by Study and Faith," *Ensign*, Feb. 2017, 59; emphasis added.

11. Oaks, "Opposition in All Things," *Ensign*, May 2016, 117.

12. Maxwell, *Meek and Lowly*, 60–61.

13. Packer, *That All May Be Edified*, 338.

14. Maxwell, "Meeting the Challenges of Today," 149; emphasis added.

15. Maxwell, *Things As They Really Are*, 73.

16. Eyring, "Finding Safety in Counsel," *Ensign*, May 1997, 25; emphasis added.

17. Monson, "Priesthood Power," *Ensign*, May 2011, 66.

18. Monson, "Choices," *Ensign*, May 2016, 86; emphasis added.

19. Maxwell, *Things As They Really Are*, 77–78; emphasis added.

20. Maxwell, *All These Things Shall Give Thee Experience*, 110.

21. McGrath, *Knowing Christ*, 79–81.

22. Uchtdorf, "Come, Join with Us," *Ensign*, Nov. 2013, 23, 24.

Chapter 6: What Faith Is Not

1. Tanner, "Basis for Faith in the Living God," *Ensign*, Nov. 1978, 46.

2. *Lectures on Faith*, 3.

3. *Lectures on Faith*, 38.

4. McConkie, *New Witness for the Articles of Faith*, 166.

5. Young, as paraphrased in Lee, *Stand Ye in Holy Places*, 163; see also Brigham Young, in *Journal of Discourses*, 9:150.

6. *Lectures on Faith*, 13.

7. Hinckley, *Faith*, 1, 5–6.

8. *Howard W. Hunter*, 272–73. Elder Jeffrey R. Holland offered inspired counsel to Brigham Young University students when he pointed them toward a life of faith, encouraging them to look forward to the future and not allow themselves to become prisoners of their past, in *To My Friends*, 143–53.

9. Maxwell, *Plain and Precious Things*, 4.
10. Mason, *Planted*, 72.
11. Nibley, *World and the Prophets*, 134; emphasis added.
12. Oaks, "Good, Better, Best," *Ensign*, Nov. 2007, 104, 107.

CHAPTER 7: WHAT FAITH IS

1. Muggeridge, *Jesus, the Man Who Lives*, 20.
2. Muggeridge, *Jesus, the Man Who Lives*, 19–20.
3. *Lectures on Faith*, 59.
4. Maxwell, *We Will Prove Them Herewith*, 72; emphasis in original.
5. Oscarson, "Do I Believe?" *Ensign*, May 2016, 88.
6. *Joseph Smith*, 266.
7. Uchtdorf, "Come, Join with Us," *Ensign*, Nov. 2013, 22.
8. Miller, *Letters to a Young Mormon*, 28–29; emphasis added.
9. *Howard W. Hunter*, 269.

CHAPTER 8: THE TRIAL OF OUR FAITH

1. See Bednar, "Always Retain a Remission of Your Sins," *Ensign*, May 2016, 59–62.
2. Maxwell, *Not My Will, but Thine*, 129.
3. *Lectures on Faith*, 68; emphasis added.
4. *Lectures on Faith*, 68.
5. *Lectures on Faith*, 69; emphasis added.
6. *Lectures on Faith*, 70.
7. Madsen, *The Highest in Us*, 49; emphasis added.
8. See *Lectures on Faith*, 69–70. Compare how Joseph Smith gained the promise of eternal life in D&C 132:49–50.
9. Bednar, "Accepting the Lord's Will and Timing," *Ensign*, Aug. 2016, 29; emphasis added.
10. Maxwell, *If Thou Endure It Well*, 54.
11. *Teachings of Thomas S. Monson*, 108.

CHAPTER 9: "ALL THINGS SHALL WORK TOGETHER"

1. Madsen, *Four Essays on Love*, 82–83.
2. Madsen, *Four Essays on Love*, 76.
3. Eyring, "Things Will Work Out," address delivered at the funeral of President Gordon B. Hinckley, 2 Feb. 2008, in *Ensign* supplement, Mar. 2008, 26, 28; emphasis added.
4. Marriott, "Yielding Our Hearts to God," *Ensign*, Nov. 2015, 31.
5. *Random House College Dictionary*, s.v. "diligent."
6. Mason, *Planted*, 80.
7. Mason, *Planted*, 80.
8. Ballard, "Opportunities and Responsibilities of CES Teachers."
9. Maxwell, "Repentance," *Ensign*, Nov. 1991, 31.
10. *Teachings of Thomas S. Monson*, 225; emphasis added.
11. *Teachings of Gordon B. Hinckley*, 468.
12. *Teachings of Gordon B. Hinckley*, 469–70.

13. Marriott, "Yielding Our Hearts to God," *Ensign*, Nov. 2015, 32.

CHAPTER 10: "WHAT GREATER WITNESS . . . ?"

1. Jensen, "Have I Received an Answer from the Spirit?" *Ensign*, Apr. 1989, 21–22.
2. Smith, *Personal Writings of Joseph Smith*, 14; spelling and punctuation modernized; emphasis added.
3. *Joseph Fielding Smith*, 183–84; see also Smith, *Doctrines of Salvation*, 1:47–48.
4. *Joseph Smith*, 121. Indeed, the Prophet offered far more caution than recommendation when it came to the gift of tongues: to be careful lest they be deceived (*Joseph Smith*, 383); that it is not necessary for tongues to be taught to the Church (*Joseph Smith*, 383); the devil will often take advantage of the innocent and unwary, and so if anything is taught in the Church by the gift of tongues, it is not to be received as doctrine (*Joseph Smith*, 384); it is the smallest gift of all but the one most sought after ("Gift of the Holy Ghost," *Times and Seasons* 3 [June 1842]: 825).
5. "Gift of the Holy Ghost," *Times and Seasons* 3 (June 1842): 825.
6. Amasa Potter, in *Joseph Smith*, 117.
7. Lee, *Stand Ye in Holy Places*, 92.
8. Packer, *That All May Be Edified*, 333–35.
9. Jensen, "Remember and Perish Not," *Ensign*, May 2007, 36.
10. Givens and Givens, *Crucible of Doubt*, 116–17; emphasis added.
11. Holland, *Trusting Jesus*, 170–72; emphasis added.
12. *Joseph Smith*, 98.
13. Benson, *Come unto Christ*, 23.
14. Covey, "An Educated Conscience," 131.

CHAPTER 11: "LORD, TO WHOM SHALL WE GO?"

1. In Andrus and Andrus, *They Knew the Prophet*, 54.
2. Maxwell, "Becometh As a Child," *Ensign*, May 1996, 68.
3. Pascal, *Pensées and Other Writings*, 156.
4. James, *Varieties of Religious Experience*, 485–86.
5. McGrath, *Doubting*, 27.
6. Shoemaker, in Gordon, *Wonder*, 130–31; emphasis added.
7. See, for example, Maxwell, "A Brother Offended," *Ensign*, May 1982, 38; "Jesus, the Perfect Mentor," *Ensign*, Feb. 2001, 13.
8. Holland, "Lord, I Believe," *Ensign*, May 2013, 94.
9. Andersen, "It's True, Isn't It? Then What Else Matters?" *Ensign*, May 2007, 72–73; emphasis added.
10. Andersen, "Faith Is Not by Chance, but by Choice," *Ensign*, Nov. 2015, 65.
11. Andersen, "Faith Is Not by Chance, but by Choice," *Ensign*, Nov. 2015, 66; emphasis added. Elder Andersen references Adam Kotter, "When Doubts and Questions Arise," *Ensign*, Mar. 2015, 37–39.
12. Maxwell, "Be of Good Cheer," *Ensign*, Nov. 1982, 68.

SOURCES

Andersen, Neil L. "Faith Is Not by Chance, but by Choice." *Ensign*, Nov. 2015, 65–68.

———. "It's True, Isn't It? Then What Else Matters?" *Ensign*, May 2007, 74–75.

Andrus, Hyrum L., and Helen Mae Andrus. *They Knew the Prophet*. Salt Lake City: Bookcraft, 1974.

Asay, Carlos E. "Salt of the Earth: Savor of Men and Saviors of Men." *Ensign*, May 1980, 42–44.

Ballard, M. Russell. "The Opportunities and Responsibilities of CES Teachers in the 21st Century." Address to religious educators, Salt Lake City, Utah, 26 Feb. 2016, https://www.lds.org/broadcasts/article/evening-with-a-general-authority/2016/02/the-opportunities-and-responsibilities-of-ces-teachers-in-the-21st-century.

Bednar, David A. "Accepting the Lord's Will and Timing." *Ensign*, Aug. 2016, 29–35.

———. "Always Retain a Remission of Your Sins." *Ensign*, May 2016, 59–62.

Benson, Ezra Taft. *Come unto Christ*. Salt Lake City: Deseret Book, 1983.

Carter, Stephen L. *The Culture of Disbelief: How American Law and Politics Trivialize Religious Devotion*. New York: HarperCollins, 1993.

Christofferson, D. Todd. "The Doctrine of Christ." *Ensign*, May 2012, 86–90.

Clayton, L. Whitney. "Rooted in Christ." *Ensign*, Aug. 2016, 16–22.

Covey, Stephen R. "An Educated Conscience." *1975 BYU Speeches of the Year*. Provo, Utah: Brigham Young University Press, 1976.

Creasy-Dean, Kenda. *Almost Christian: What the Faith of Our Teenagers Is Telling the American Church*. New York: Oxford University Press, 2010.

The Death of God Debate. Edited by Jackson Lee Ice and John J. Cary. Philadelphia: Westminster Press, 1967.

Erekson, Keith A. "Understanding Church History by Study and Faith." *Ensign*, Feb. 2017, 56–59.

Eyring, Henry B. "Eyes to See, Ears to Hear." *Eighth Annual Church Educational System Religious Educators' Symposium*. Salt Lake City: The Church of Jesus Christ of Latter-day Saints, 1984; available online at https://si.lds.org/library /talks/ces-symposium-addresses/eyes-to-see-ears-to-hear?lang=eng.

———. "Finding Safety in Counsel." *Ensign*, May 1997, 24–26.

———. "Things Will Work Out." Address delivered at the funeral of President Gordon B. Hinckley, 2 Feb. 2008. *Ensign* supplement, Mar. 2008, 26–28.

Fletcher, Joseph. *Situation Ethics: The New Morality*. Philadelphia: Westminster Press, 1966.

Givens, Terryl L., and Fiona Givens. *The Crucible of Doubt: Reflections on the Quest for Faith*. Salt Lake City: Deseret Book, 2014.

Givens, Terryl L., and Matthew J. Grow. *Parley P. Pratt: The Apostle Paul of Mormonism*. New York: Oxford University Press, 2011.

Gordon, Arthur. *Wonder: Moments That Keep You Falling in Love with Life*. Grand Rapids, Mich.: Revell, 1974.

Hinckley, Gordon B. *Faith, the Essence of True Religion*. Salt Lake City: Deseret Book, 1989.

———. "Find the Lambs, Feed the Sheep." *Ensign*, May 1999, 104–10.

———. *Teachings of Gordon B. Hinckley*. Salt Lake City: Deseret Book, 1997.

Holland, Jeffrey R. "Lord, I Believe." *Ensign*, May 2013, 93–95.

———. *To My Friends: Counsel and Comfort from Jeffrey R. Holland*. Salt Lake City: Deseret Book, 2014.

———. *Trusting Jesus*. Salt Lake City: Deseret Book, 2003.

———, and Patricia T. Holland. *On Earth As It Is in Heaven*. Salt Lake City: Deseret Book, 1989.

Hunter, Howard W. *The Teachings of Howard W. Hunter*. Edited by Clyde J. Williams. Salt Lake City: Bookcraft, 1997.

———. *Howard W. Hunter*. Teachings of Presidents of the Church series. Salt Lake City: The Church of Jesus Christ of Latter-day Saints, 2015.

Hymns of The Church of Jesus Christ of Latter-day Saints. Salt Lake City: The Church of Jesus Christ of Latter-day Saints, 1985.

James, William. *The Varieties of Religious Experience: A Study in Human Nature*. Edited by Martin E. Marty. New York: Penguin Books, 1982.

Jensen, Jay E. "Have I Received an Answer from the Spirit?" *Ensign*, Apr. 1989, 20–25.

Jensen, Marlin K. "Remember and Perish Not." *Ensign*, May 2007, 36–38.

Jorgensen, Lynne Watkins. "The Mantle of the Prophet Joseph Passes to Brother Brigham: One Hundred Twenty-one Testimonies of a Collective Spiritual Witness." In *Opening the Heavens: Accounts of Divine Manifestations, 1820–1844*, edited by John W. Welch and Erick B. Carlson, 373–407. Provo, Utah, and Salt Lake City: Brigham Young University Press and Deseret Book, 2005.

Journal of Discourses. 26 vols. Liverpool: F. D. Richards & Sons, 1851–86.

Kimball, Spencer W. "Listen to the Prophets." *Ensign*, May 1978, 76–78.

Kolodiejchuk, Brian, ed. *Mother Teresa: Come Be My Light; The Private Writings of the Saint of Calcutta*. New York: Random House, 2007.

Kotter, Adam. "When Doubts and Questions Arise." *Ensign*, Mar. 2015, 37–39.

Lectures on Faith. Salt Lake City: Deseret Book, 1985.

Lee, Harold B. *Stand Ye in Holy Places*. Salt Lake City: Deseret Book, 1974.

———. *Teachings of Harold B. Lee*. Edited by Clyde J. Williams. Salt Lake City: Bookcraft, 1996.

Lewis, C. S. *Mere Christianity*. New York: Touchstone, 1996.

MacArthur, John. *The Vanishing Conscience*. Dallas: Word Publishing, 1994.

Madsen, Truman G. *Four Essays on Love*. Salt Lake City: Deseret Book, 1971.

———. *The Highest in Us*. Salt Lake City: Bookcraft, 1978.

Marriott, Neill F. "Yielding Our Hearts to God." *Ensign*, Nov. 2015, 30–32.

Mason, Patrick. *Planted: Belief and Belonging in an Age of Doubt*. Salt Lake City and Provo, Utah: Deseret Book and Neal A. Maxwell Institute for Religious Scholarship, 2015.

Maxwell, Neal A. *All These Things Shall Give Thee Experience*. Salt Lake City: Deseret Book, 1979.

———. "A Brother Offended." *Ensign*, May 1982, 37–39.

———. "Be of Good Cheer." *Ensign*, Nov. 1982, 66–68.

———. "Becometh As a Child." *Ensign*, May 1996, 68–70.

———. *If Thou Endure It Well*. Salt Lake City: Deseret Book, 1996.

———. "Jesus, the Perfect Mentor." *Ensign*, Feb. 2001, 8–17.

———. *Meek and Lowly*. Salt Lake City: Deseret Book, 1987.

———. "Meeting the Challenges of Today." *1978 Devotional Speeches of the Year*, 149–56. Provo, Utah: Brigham Young University Press, 1979.

———. *Not My Will, but Thine*. Salt Lake City: Deseret Book, 1988.

———. *Notwithstanding My Weakness*. Salt Lake City: Deseret Book, 1981.

———. *Plain and Precious Things*. Salt Lake City: Deseret Book, 1983.

———. "Repentance." *Ensign*, Nov. 1991, 30–32.

———. *Things As They Really Are*. Salt Lake City: Deseret Book, 1978.

———. *We Will Prove Them Herewith*. Salt Lake City: Deseret Book, 1982.

McConkie, Bruce R. *Doctrinal New Testament Commentary*. 3 vols. Salt Lake City: Bookcraft, 1965–73.

———. *A New Witness for the Articles of Faith*. Salt Lake City: Deseret Book, 1985.

———. *The Promised Messiah*. Salt Lake City: Deseret Book, 1978.

McConkie, Joseph Fielding. "The Gathering of Israel and the Return of Christ." *Sixth Annual CES Religious Educators' Symposium*, 3–5. Salt Lake City: The Church of Jesus Christ of Latter-day Saints, 1982.

McConkie, Joseph Fielding, and Robert L. Millet. *Sustaining and Defending the Faith*. Salt Lake City: Bookcraft, 1985.

McDowell, Josh, and Bob Hostetler. *Right from Wrong*. Dallas: Word Publishing, 1994.

McGrath, Alister. *Doubting: Growing through the Uncertainties of Faith*. Downers Grove, Ill.: IVP Books, 2006.

———. *Knowing Christ*. New York: Doubleday, 2002.

McKay, David. O. In Conference Report, Apr. 1907, 10–14.

———. In Conference Report, Apr. 1962, 5–9.

Miller, Adam S. *Letters to a Young Mormon*. Provo, Utah: Neal A. Maxwell Institute for Religious Scholarship, 2014.

Millet, Robert L., ed. *No Weapon Shall Prosper: New Light on Sensitive Issues*. Salt Lake City and Provo, Utah: Deseret Book and BYU Religious Studies Center, 2011.

Mohler, R. Albert, Jr. *Atheism Remix: A Christian Confronts the New Atheists*. Wheaton, Ill.: Crossway Books, 2008.

Monson, Thomas S. "Choices." *Ensign*, May 2016, 86.

———. "Priesthood Power." *Ensign*, May 2011, 66–69.

———. *Teachings of Thomas S. Monson*. Compiled by Lynne F. Cannegieter. Salt Lake City: Deseret Book, 2011.

Moore, Richard G. *Strange Roads and Forbidden Paths: Avoiding Apostasy in the Latter Days*. Springville, Utah: CFI, 2008.

Muggeridge, Malcolm. *Jesus, the Man Who Lives*. New York: Collins, 1975.

Nash, Marcus B. "Guided Safely Home." Brigham Young University devotional address, 2 Feb. 2016, ; available online at speeches.byu.edu.

The New Shorter Oxford English Dictionary. Edited by Lesley Brown. 2 vols. Oxford: Clarendon Press, 1993.

Nibley, Hugh W. *The World and the Prophets*. Salt Lake City and Provo, Utah: Deseret Book and FARMS (Foundation for Ancient Research and Mormon Studies), 1987.

Oaks, Dallin H. "Opposition in All Things." *Ensign*, May 2016, 114–17.

———. "Good, Better, Best." *Ensign*, November 2007, 104–8.

Oscarson, Bonnie L. "Do I Believe?" *Ensign*, May 2016, 87–89.

Packer, Boyd K. "The Great Plan of Happiness." *Seventeenth Annual CES Religious Educators' Symposium*. Salt Lake City: The Church of Jesus Christ of Latter-day Saints, 1993; available online at https://si.lds.org/library/talks/ces-symposium-addresses/the-great-plan-of-happiness?lang=eng.

———. "Little Children." *Ensign*, Nov. 1986, 16–18.

———. *That All May Be Edified*. Salt Lake City: Bookcraft, 1982.

Pascal, Blaise. *Pensées and Other Writings*. Translated by Honor Levi. New York: Oxford University Press, 1995.

Penrose, Charles W. In Conference Report, Oct. 1911, 47–54.

Peterson, Eugene. *The Message: The Bible in Contemporary Language*. Colorado Springs, Colo.: NavPress, 2002.

The Random House College Dictionary. Edited by Jess Stein. Rev. ed. New York: Random House, 1983.

Rasband, Ronald A. "Standing with the Leaders of the Church." *Ensign*, May 2016, 46–49.

Roberts, B. H. *The Life of John Taylor*. Salt Lake City: Bookcraft, 1963.

Robinson, John A. T. *Honest to God*. Philadelphia: Westminster Press, 1963.

Smith, Christian, and Melinda Lundquist Denton. *Soul Searching: The Religious and Spiritual Lives of American Teenagers*. New York: Oxford University Press, 2005.

Smith, George Albert. *The Teachings of George Albert Smith*. Compiled by Robert and McIntosh and Susan McIntosh. Salt Lake City: Bookcraft, 1996.

Smith, Joseph. *Personal Writings of Joseph Smith*. Edited by Dean C. Jessee. Rev. ed. Salt Lake City: Deseret Book, 2002.

———. *Joseph Smith*. Teachings of Presidents of the Church series. Salt Lake City: The Church of Jesus Christ of Latter-day Saints, 2007.

———. *The Words of Joseph Smith: The Contemporary Accounts of the Nauvoo Discourses of the Prophet Joseph*. Edited by Andrew F. Ehat and Lyndon W. Cook. Provo, Utah: Brigham Young University Religious Studies Center, 1980.

Smith, Joseph F. *Gospel Doctrine*. Salt Lake City: Deseret Book, 1971.

Smith, Joseph Fielding. *Doctrines of Salvation*. 3 vols. Compiled by Bruce R. McConkie. Salt Lake City: Bookcraft, 1954–56.

———. *Joseph Fielding Smith*. Teachings of Presidents of the Church series. Salt Lake City: The Church of Jesus Christ of Latter-day Saints, 2013.

———. *Take Heed to Yourselves*. Salt Lake City: Deseret Book, 1971.

Sykes, Charles. *A Nation of Victims*. New York: St. Martin's Press, 1992.

Tanner, N. Eldon. "A Basis for Faith in the Living God." *Ensign*, Nov. 1978, 46–49.

Taylor, Charles. *A Secular Age*. Cambridge: Harvard University Press, 2007.

Uchtdorf, Dieter F. "Come, Join with Us." *Ensign*, Nov. 2013, 21–24.

———. "It Works Wonderfully!" *Ensign*, Nov. 2015, 20–23.

Webster, Noah. *An American Dictionary of the English Language*. Facsimile ed. San Francisco: Foundation for American Christian Education, 1985.

Whitney, Orson F. *Life of Heber C. Kimball*. Salt Lake City: Bookcraft, 1973.

Widtsoe, John A. *Evidences and Reconciliations*. Salt Lake City: Bookcraft, 1960.

Wilson, James Q. *The Moral Sense*. New York: Macmillan, 1993.

Wright, N. T. *The Kingdom New Testament: A Contemporary Translation*. New York: Harper Collins, 2011.

Young, Brigham. *Brigham Young*. Teachings of Presidents of the Church series. Salt Lake City: The Church of Jesus Christ of Latter-day Saints, 1997.

INDEX